THE MICROWAVE
WHOLEFOOD
COOKBOOK

THE MICROWAVE
WHOLEFOOD
COOKBOOK

Val Collins

DAVID & CHARLES
Newton Abbot   London   North Pomfret (Vt)

Acknowledgements

I should like to express my sincere thanks to Rosemary Moon for all the test work she has carried out and for helping me with the food for photography. Thanks also to Thorn EMI Major Domestic Appliances Limited for supplying microwave cookers.
Photography by John Plimmer, RPM Photographic, Havant, Hants.
Line illustrations by Mona Thorogood.

British Library Cataloguing in Publication Data

Collins, Val
    The microwave wholefood cookbook.
    1. Cookery (Natural foods)   2. Microwave
    cookery
    I. Title
    641.5'637   TX741

    ISBN 0-7153-8691-3

Phototypeset by ABM Typographics Limited, Hull
and printed in The Netherlands
by Smeets Offset BV, Weert
for David & Charles (Publishers) Limited
Brunel House   Newton Abbot   Devon

Published in the United States of America
by David & Charles Inc
North Pomfret   Vermont 05053   USA

Contents

Introduction

As a confirmed devotee of the microwave cooker, I am always impressed when unknowing friends and acquaintances remark on the delicious results presented to them for sampling. It might be something I have created for a lunch or dinner party, or a last-minute snack rustled up for an unexpected visitor. But as someone who is often expected to serve something special, I confess that I am still delighted to hear the 'oohs' and 'aahs', and am sure I share this delight with all those who are interested in cooking. Unfortunately I cannot take all the credit because the microwave cooker does produce better, tastier food. Gone are the days when the microwave was used merely for defrosting frozen goods and reheating ready prepared foods. Certainly it does those jobs efficiently, but it has so much more to offer in the preparation of fresh foods and is a valuable aid to healthy eating.

Over the past few years the link between good eating and good health has been well established, and there is now a greater awareness of the importance of eating wholesome natural foods. Commercial foods in cans and packets have lost much of their natural goodness in the refining process and instead contain chemicals in the forms of additives, preservatives, colouring and flavouring to make them easy to cook and eat, but far from nutritious. In these busy days of rush and hurry, time—or lack of it—is one of the main reasons given why not everyone is switching to a healthy eating plan. This is where the microwave cooker comes in, and where the full potential of this adaptable and flexible kitchen appliance is finally recognised.

With its speed of cooking and the fact that foods can be cooked in their own juices, the microwave cooker scores nutritionally over probably most other cooking methods. All natural flavours, textures and colours are retained, and reduced cooking times cut down losses of valuable trace elements, vitamin C and fragile B vitamins. Many foods can be cooked without additional fat—important for low cholestrol diets and excellent for slimmers. In addition, the microwave cooker is ideal for reheating foods quickly and efficiently for someone late home for a meal, without the dangers of food drying out and with the certainty of preserving freshly cooked flavours and colours. It eliminates the necessity of keeping food hot in a warming cupboard or oven, which can destroy heat sensitive nutrients and does absolutely nothing to please the eye, let alone the palate.

For the experienced user, the advantages the microwave cooker gives can be difficult to recall; you begin to take for granted that it is safe to use and energy efficient. Microwave cookers are also easy to instal and operate, portable and easy to clean! So, those of you interested in a healthy eating plan, use your versatile, convenient microwave cooker and the wholefood recipes in this book to produce quick, tastier food and prepare delicious, healthy meals for family and friends. I'm sure you will be delighted with the results.

Ratatouille (page 93); Banana Salad (page 92); Cheese and Vegetable Dip (page 40); Light German Pumpernickel (page 112); Pressed Tongue (page 65); Pheasant and Chicken Terrine (page 65)

Microwave cooking techniques

Cooking by microwave does not mean learning completely new techniques, but there are some special considerations which help to ensure successful results. The operating instructions supplied with your cooker or a book on basic microwave cooking will give all the details you will need, but the following few reminders of the factors and terms to watch for may be worthwhile.

Starting temperature

Allowances must be made when using food straight from the refrigerator, as differences in the temperature of the food when placed in the microwave will affect the length of cooking time required. The colder the food, the longer it will take to cook.

Density and texture

As microwave cooking is so fast, differences in density and texture will show up more quickly in the end result. A lighter mixture will cook or reheat faster, as it allows microwave energy to penetrate more easily than a heavier one.

Moisture

Moisture, too, can affect cooking times as microwave energy reacts mainly on water molecules. Some of the recipes in this book have been adjusted to use more or less liquid than you are perhaps used to in order to ensure successful results.

Seasonings

Salt can have a toughening effect, especially on meat and poultry, so use minimal seasoning during the cooking process and adjust the seasoning to taste at the finish.

Covering foods

When cooking conventionally, lids on dishes or saucepans assist the food to heat through more quickly; it is the same when cooking in the microwave. Whether a lid on a casserole dish is used or food is covered with clingfilm, the steam is trapped inside and this will enable even and slightly faster results to be obtained. Covering food also allows minimal liquid to be used and ensures no flavour loss.

Quantity

As the quantity of food placed in the oven is increased, the length of cooking time also needs to be increased proportionately. Similarly, if you use less than the quantities given in the recipe, the cooking times should be adjusted accordingly.

Arrangement of food

When heating or cooking a number of similar items together, they should be of even size where possible and arranged in a circle on a plate or on the cooking shelf.

Stirring and turning

Stirring during a heating or cooking process is recommended in some dishes to ensure an even distribution of heat. When it is not possible to stir, particularly when cooking large, whole items, simply rearrange the dish in the oven cavity by giving it a half or quarter turn. This is not always necessary if a microwave cooker with a turntable is used.

Standing times

All foods continue cooking to a degree when removed from the oven and some dishes will require this standing or resting period to assist with the heating or cooking process.

Utensils

Microwave energy is reflected from metal which means that aluminium foil, aluminium, tin, copper and stainless steel containers must not be used. However, microwave energy passes through glass, pottery, heatproof plastics and china and so, provided that they have no metal trim, these are all excellent containers for use in the microwave. Some pottery and china absorb more microwave energy which makes them less efficient. Remember that generally, the more regular the shape of the container, the better it is for even heating or cooking. A wide choice of special microwave cooking containers and utensils is available now, but a selection would depend on your needs and preferences. Some of these dishes are intended for both microwave and conventional cooker as well as the freezer, which is an added advantage.

Browning dishes

These are specially designed for use in the microwave cooker. In appearance they are normal glass ceramic dishes but have a special coating in the base. When the dish is preheated in the microwave, the base absorbs microwave energy and gets very hot. Food such as steak, chicken portions, bacon or chops are placed on the hot base which sears the outside of the food, similar to grilling or frying, while microwave energy cooks the food.

Aluminium foil

The narrow ends of fish, meat and poultry may be wrapped in small, smooth pieces of aluminium foil for part of the heating or cooking time to protect them from overcooking. Care should be taken to ensure the foil is smoothed tightly around the ends, and it must not be allowed to touch the interior surfaces of the microwave oven cavity. Always check with your manufacturer's instructions with reference to the use of aluminium foil in your particular model.

Variable power settings

Different manufacturers portray the variable power settings on the control panels of their models in different ways. It is useful to compare these in chart form to enable you to adapt the cooking times given in this book to suit your particular model, but do check your microwave cooker instructions with reference to the description of settings related to the percentage and power inputs.

1 Keep Warm LOW 150W 20–25%	2 Simmer DEFROST 200W 30%	3 Stew MEDIUM-LOW 250W 40%	4 Defrost MEDIUM 300W 50%	5 Bake MEDIUM-HIGH 400W 60%	6 Roast HIGH 500W 75%	7 High FULL 650W 100%

Power levels and timings

By using the chart given below, it is possible to adapt the cooking times given in this book to suit your own particular model. However, the timings given in the chart are intended as a guide only, as much depends on the shape, density, texture and temperature of the food. The calculations have been based on a microwave cooker with an average power output of 650 watts and, of course, this may vary between different models. Allow slightly more time if using a microwave cooker with a lower output and slightly less time if using a cooker with a higher output.

		10%	20%	30%	40%	50%	60%	70%	80%	90%	100%
	1	10	5	3¼	2½	2	1¾	1½	1¼	1	1
	2	20	10	7	5	4	3¼	2¾	2½	2¼	2
	3	30	15	10	7½	6	5	4	3¾	3¼	3
Cooking	4	40	20	13	10	8	7	5¼	5	4¾	4
time	5	50	25	17	12	10	8	7	6	5½	5
(minutes)	6	60	30	20	15	12	10	8	7½	6½	6
	7	70	35	23	17	14	12	9¼	8¾	7¾	7
	8	80	40	27	20	16	13	11	10	9	8
	9	90	45	30	22	18	15	12	11	10	9
	10	100	50	33	25	20	16	13	12	11	10

For times greater than 10 min, add together the figures in the appropriate columns.

Wholefoods in the diet

A wholefood diet is one which incorporates a selection of fresh, natural or 'whole' foods to give our bodies the balanced requirements of proteins, carbohydrates, fats, vitamins and minerals, and avoids manufactured or processed foods containing additives and preservatives. It should not be regarded as a here-today-gone-tomorrow 'fad', as too many popular diets are, but should be introduced gradually over a period of time until a healthy eating pattern becomes a way of life. The aim is to build up an insurance against diseases which have increased to alarming proportions in the modern western world—obesity, heart disease, dental decay are just a few which have been linked to non-selective eating habits—and to promote a healthier, fitter, more energetic lifestyle.

The popular belief that wholefoods are expensive is without much justification. Consider the value-for-money wholefood ingredients which may already feature as part of the weekly shop—eggs, cheese, fish, pulses, fresh vegetables and fruits. Compare these food items with the same variety of commercially prepared food packs available. By reading the labels you will soon see the difference and, once you have stocked up, you may even find that eating wholefoods can work out cheaper. Next time you go shopping, as you stop and peruse, give a little thought to buying 'fresh' and you will be on the way to a healthy, wholefood diet.

Butter Bean Bourguinon (page 73); Red Cabbage with Fennel (page 96); Celery with Herbs and Lemon (page 92); Cashew and Walnut Cutlets (page 81)

Eggs

Eggs are particularly nourishing and provide first-class protein. They are easy to prepare and extremely versatile in that they lend themselves to a variety of

different dishes. Free-range eggs, although a little more expensive, are worthwhile buying and are gradually becoming available in more high street shops.

Dairy products

These include milk, cream, yoghurt and cheese. Milk is a complete food containing protein, fats and carbohydrates and its use in the kitchen is almost endless. Dried milk powder and skimmed milks have a lighter effect in cooking and are lower in fat content than ordinary milks. Double and thick cream may be replaced by the lighter soured cream and yoghurt which is particularly good, having virtually the same nutritional value as milk. From the wide choice of cheese available, look for the lower-fat curd and cottage cheeses. Medium-fat cream cheese and hard cheese such as edam can be used occasionally and, of the traditional english cheddars, try the farmhouse varieties, as they have the best flavour and you need use less at one time.

Fish

Fish is high in protein and rich in minerals. Choose from white fish, oily fish or shellfish as all varieties are available to the wholefood cook. Most fishmongers have an excellent source of fresh fish delivered daily and offer good value for money, although it may be necessary to save some of the more expensive shellfish for special occasions only!

Meat

Meat is a first-class protein, rich in vitamins and minerals. The wholefood cook should try to find a regular supply of meat which has been naturally reared, perhaps from a nearby farm or through a known local butcher. Alternatively, game is an obvious natural form of meat and is increasing in popularity as a basic wholefood.

Vegetables and fruits

Vegetables and fruits are the wholefooder's delight, providing a complete selection of vitamins and minerals but across the varieties, so it is best to buy a selection of different ones in small quantities at a time. Use them up quickly as they are all the better for being absolutely fresh and learn to serve them in adventurous ways, as a feature of the meal rather than an insignificant side dish.

Bread

The increasing popularity of bread made with 100% wholewheat flour has made it easily available at bakers' shops and supermarkets. You will find that you will need less of it as it contains fibre—as well as valuable nutrients—so it's far more satisfying than white bread. Make sure you buy real wholewheat bread rather than the brown bread made from dyed, refined white flour.

Pulses

Dried peas, beans and lentils are all pulses and have a high proportion of carbohydrates as well as B vitamins, calcium, iron and potassium. They are not so high in protein, but the addition of other ingredients will increase their value. There is a tremendous variety available—some of the most popular ones are in many high street supermarkets—and they are extremely versatile in cooking.

Grains

Grains such as barley, wheat, rye, bulgar wheat, millet, buckwheat, oats and brown rice are inexpensive, versatile and nutritious containing protein, vitamins and minerals as well as carbohydrate. They are extremely satisfying and are often used to provide the 'filling' part of the wholefood menu. You will find the best selection of grains in healthfood shops, although some supermarkets now have a few varieties on sale.

Nuts and seeds

These are both high-energy foods and rich sources of protein, so should be used in limited amounts. Their vitamin content is mainly A and B group plus a high level of minerals and, as such, they are very nutritious. Nuts in particular are best combined with other ingredients such as breadcrumbs, vegetables, salads and pulses to make a variety of wholefood dishes. Freshly shelled nuts have the best flavour, but the already shelled varieties are often more convenient to use in the kitchen.

Fats and oils

Both fats and oils should be kept to a minimum in a wholefood diet, especially the animal fats in egg yolks, cheese, butter, hard margarine, lard and meat. However, these are natural foods and, if used sparingly, will cause no harm when combined with other wholefoods such as fresh vegetables and fruits and alternative protein foods. Vegetable oils such as sunflower, safflower, corn and olive should be used as necessary for general cooking purposes but, when baking, sunflower margarine is a useful substitute for butter.

Flour

100% unrefined wholewheat flour contains essential nutrients and fibre and is the best for general wholefood cooking. Use it for thickening sauces and soups, and most bread, scones and pastry can be made using this flour; but until you get used to the coarser texture, you may find that the finer 81% wholewheat flour is preferable.

Sugar

Unrefined raw cane sugars such as demerara or muscovado are the ones to look for, and if the packet states the country of origin you can be sure it's the real product and not a refined white sugar which has been processed. Alternative sweeteners are honey, molasses and maple syrup. Artificial sweeteners are as their name implies, and have no place in a wholefood diet.

Dried fruits

Many different sorts of dried fruits are now available and are a concentrated form of goodness, more so even than fresh fruits. Eat them as they are instead of sweets, cook them for use in 'winter' fruit salads, mix them into savoury salads, add them to stuffings or use them in baking as a natural sweetener.

Soya products

Tofu is a soya bean curd similar in appearance to dairy milk curd made by adding rennet. It may be used in many different ways as a protein food and is often sliced and added to stir-fry dishes. Tamari sauce is a soy sauce but with a superior, richer flavour. It is made from soya beans and sea salt, and is mainly available from healthfood shops. Miso is made from fermented soya beans and is in the form of a thick paste. It can be added to meatless dishes for additional protein and flavour. Soya flour is often added to cake and bread recipes for extra protein. Soya milk is also available, and is a useful substitute for anyone allergic to cow's milk.

About freezing

A wholefood diet is based on eating freshly cooked natural foods, but frozen foods can be allowed occasionally without too much harm to your healthy eating plan. Generally, freezing your own fresh wholefoods is ideal, but will give some nutrient loss which becomes greater the longer the foods are stored. All foods must be frozen quickly otherwise large ice crystals will form and vitamins will be lost on thawing.

Commercially prepared frozen goods may contain additives, depending on the variety. For example, some fruits may be chemically treated to retain colour and flavour, whereas frozen vegetables generally contain no additives but are subjected to preparation and blanching before the freezing process. Fish freezes well and by law is additive free, although some fish is coated in batter or coloured breadcrumbs and should therefore be excluded from the wholefood diet. Frozen unprepared meat is also additive free but is inclined to lose some nutrients during storage, and oven-ready frozen poultry may well be treated with chemicals to retard bacterial growth and to prevent water loss during cooking.

The best plan of action is to ensure that the foods stored in your freezer are your own home-frozen ones. Enthusiasts may well grow their own fruits and vegetables which makes sure of absolute freshness for picking and freezing. The big advantage of defrosting food by microwave is that it is so fast compared with conventional methods that there is less flavour loss, and risk of bacterial growth is minimal by comparison.

Defrosting by microwave

This is usually carried out using a low 30% or 50% power level, which allows either a reduced wattage or a pulsed energy cycle into the microwave oven

Beef with Mango (page 64); Hazelnut Pâté (page 84)

14

cavity to ensure an even thaw and prevent food from cooking. You can check whether food is defrosted by feel or by using a thermometer. When defrosting some larger food items, extra standing periods may be required to give a perfect thaw and to ensure that the food is at an even temperature throughout before it is subsequently cooked. Always refer to the manufacturer's instructions and be guided by their recommendations, although experience will help you to determine which methods suit you best.

Important reminders

★ All cooking is carried out in the microwave cooker using 100% (full) power unless otherwise stated. Some microwave cooking instructions are given for models with variable power control settings, but it is still possible to cook the dish on models without this facility by referring to the Power Level Chart on page 10 and calculating the time required for cooking on 100% (full) power. The automatic intermittent 'off' periods can be achieved manually by allowing the dish to rest at 1–2 min intervals throughout the cooking duration.

★ Metal baking tins or metal-trimmed dishes must not be used in the microwave cooker.

★ The recommended cooking times are intended as a guide only as so much depends on the power input to the microwave oven cavity; the shape, material and size of the dish; the temperature of the food at the commencement of cooking, and the depth of food in the dish.

★ If the quantities of food placed in the cooker are increased or decreased, then the cooking times must be adjusted accordingly.

★ Always undercook rather than overcook the food by cooking for a little less time than the recipe recommends, allowing the extra time if required.

★ When reheating or cooking foods, best results are obtained if the food is at an even temperature throughout—particularly important when cooking foods after defrosting.

★ Some foods, ie casseroles, require stirring during defrosting, reheating or cooking to assist with the heating process. After cooking with microwave energy, heat equalisation or standing time is often recommended. This allows the distribution of heat evenly throughout the food.

★ Deep-fat frying must not be attempted as the temperature of the oil or fat cannot be controlled.

★ Microwave cooking does not brown some food in the traditional way, but dishes can be finished off in a conventional oven or under a grill if required. Where appropriate I have included recipes for microwave/conventional cooking for those of you who may prefer traditional browning.

Soups and Sauces

Soups

Home-made soups using good stock are particularly nourishing and delicious. Whether served as a starter to a meal or as a snack, a thick warming soup is always welcome on a cold winter's day and, when the weather is hot, many can also be served cold or chilled. With the addition of a garnish, the most humble soup can be turned into something a little more special. Toasted wholewheat croûtons, fresh herbs, a spoonful of soured cream or natural yoghurt, or tiny pieces of raw vegetable can all be used effectively to enhance the appearance and complement the flavour.

Soups are inexpensive to make and, when cooked in the microwave, will retain their full flavours and colours. Once cooked, individual portions may be reheated in bowls or mugs which is a great saving on washing up—one will take about 3 min and two will take about 5–5½ min.

Sauces

Sauces can be very easy to make and will improve the appearance and flavour of many basic foods and ingredients. Initially, you may consider that it is hardly worth the effort of cooking sauces in the microwave as the time saving is little but, providing it is stirred at intervals during the cooking process, the result is a very smooth sauce. One advantage is that other ingredients can be added for heating through as the sauce is cooking and, of course, there will be only one dish or bowl to wash afterwards. When a sauce is to be handed separately at the table, it can be made in advance and then quickly reheated before serving—often in the jug in which it is to be served thereby eliminating messy pans to clean.

25g (1oz) butter or sunflower
  margarine
450g (1lb) parsnips, chopped
1 onion, chopped
1 clove garlic, crushed
salt and pepper
½ × 5ml tsp (½tsp) ground
  mace
825ml (1½pt) boiling vegetable
  stock
550ml (1pt) milk
100g (4oz) walnuts, roughly
  chopped
1 × 15ml tbsp (1tbsp) chopped
  chives

Creamy parsnip and walnut soup *(serves 8)* *colour opposite*
POWER LEVEL: 100% (FULL)

1 Melt the butter or margarine in a large bowl for 1–2 min. Add the parsnips, onion and garlic. Cover and cook for 8–10 min, stirring once during cooking.
2 Add the seasoning, mace, stock and milk. Cover and cook for 10 min, then add the walnuts.
3 Purée the soup in a blender or food processor. Pour into a serving dish or tureen.
4 Adjust the seasoning and reheat for a few minutes if necessary before serving sprinkled with the chopped chives.

1 onion, chopped
½ head celery, roughly
  chopped
225g (8oz) shelled peas
550ml (1pt) boiling vegetable
  stock
salt and pepper
1 bay leaf
1 × 5ml tsp (1tsp) chopped
  mixed herbs
50g (2oz) cooked potato,
  creamed or mashed
150ml (¼pt) milk
150ml (¼pt) soured cream
for garnish: chopped parsley

Celery and pea soup *(serves 4–6)* *colour opposite*
POWER LEVEL: 100% (FULL)

1 Place the onion, celery, peas and stock in a large bowl. Add the seasoning, bay leaf and herbs, cover and cook for 12–15 min until the vegetables are tender.
2 Remove the bay leaf and allow the soup to cool slightly before puréeing in a blender or food processor. Add the mashed potato to thicken the soup.
3 Add the milk and pour the soup into a serving dish. Reheat for 3–4 min.
4 Stir in the soured cream, and sprinkle with the chopped parsley before serving.

100g (4oz) aduki beans
boiling water
2 × 15ml tbsp (2tbsp)
  sunflower oil
1 large onion, finely chopped
1 clove garlic, crushed
1 stick celery, finely chopped
1 carrot, finely diced
2 tomatoes, skinned and
  chopped
2 × 15ml tbsp (2tbsp) tomato
  paste
1 bay leaf
½ × 5ml tsp (½tsp) chilli
  powder
salt and pepper
550ml (1pt) boiling vegetable
  stock
for garnish: chopped coriander
  or parlsey

Aduki bean broth *(serves 4–6)* *colour opposite*
POWER LEVEL: 100% (FULL) AND 50%

1 Place the beans in a bowl and cover with boiling water. Cover the bowl and heat for 5 min, then leave to stand for 1 hr.
2 Drain the beans, cover with fresh boiling water and cover the dish. Cook for 10 min on 100% (full) and a further 10–15 min on 50% setting. Allow to stand.
3 Heat the oil in a large casserole dish for 2 min. Stir in the onion, garlic, celery and carrot, cover and cook for 5 min, stirring once throughout.
4 Add the tomatoes, tomato paste, herbs, seasoning, stock and the drained aduki beans. Cover and cook for 10 min. Remove the cover from the dish and cook for a further 5–10 min to slightly reduce the liquid.
5 Adjust the seasoning and serve sprinkled with the chopped coriander or parsley.

Aduki Bean Broth (above); Artichoke and Apricot Soup (page 20); Celery and Pea Soup (above); Creamy Parsnip and Walnut Soup (above)

100g (4oz) dried apricots
water
1 large onion, chopped
2 cloves garlic, crushed
450g (1lb) jerusalem
   artichokes, peeled and
   roughly chopped
salt and pepper
550ml (1pt) boiling vegetable
   stock, approximately
1 × 15ml tbsp (1tbsp) fresh
   chopped tarragon or 1 × 5ml
   tsp (1tsp) dried tarragon
½ lemon, juice
425ml (¾pt) milk
for garnish: chopped tarragon
   or parsley

Artichoke and apricot soup *(serves 6–8)*   *colour page 19*
POWER LEVEL: 100% (FULL)

1 Place the apricots in a bowl and cover with water. Cover the bowl with a lid or pierced clingfilm and heat for 5 min. Stand for 10 min.
2 Drain the apricots, reserving the liquid, and chop them roughly.
3 Cook the onion and garlic in a large covered bowl for 5 min. Add the artichokes, apricots and salt and pepper.
4 Make the apricot liquid up to 825ml (1½pt) with a vegetable stock cube and boiling water (or use freshly made vegetable stock, page 21). Add to the artichokes with the tarragon and lemon juice.
5 Cover and cook for 12–15 min until the vegetables are tender. Leave to cool slightly and purée in a blender or food processor. Add the milk and adjust the seasoning.
6 Reheat for 2–3 min before serving garnished with the chopped tarragon or parsley.

450g (1lb) carrots, sliced
3 oranges, rind and juice
1 onion, chopped
salt and pepper
1 × 5ml tsp (1tsp) grated
   nutmeg
1 × 15ml tbsp (1tbsp) fresh
   chopped mint or 1 × 5ml tsp
   (1tsp) dried mint
825ml (1½pt) boiling vegetable
   stock
sugar, dark demerara or
   muscovado to taste
1 × 15ml tbsp (1tbsp) soured
   cream

Carrot and orange soup *(serves 4)*
POWER LEVEL: 100% (FULL)

1 Place the carrots, orange rind and juice and onion in a large bowl. Cover and cook for 8–10 min, stirring once throughout.
2 Add the seasoning, nutmeg, mint and stock. Cover and cook for 10–15 min or until the carrots are tender.
3 Purée the soup in a blender or food processor. Pour into a serving dish.
4 Add sugar to taste and extra seasoning if necessary. Reheat for 2–3 min, stir in the cream and serve hot.

1 chicken carcass
1 large onion, chopped
1 carrot, diced
1 leek, sliced
1 bay leaf
salt and pepper
825ml (1½pt) boiling water
25g (1oz) flaked almonds
1 bunch watercress, washed
275ml (½pt) milk
3 × 15ml tbsp (3tbsp) soured
   cream

Creamed chicken and watercress soup *(serves 6)*
POWER LEVEL: 100% (FULL)

1 Place the chicken carcass, onion, carrot, leek, bay leaf and seasoning in a large bowl. Add the boiling water, cover the bowl and cook for 15–20 min. Leave to cool.
2 Place the almonds on a heatproof plate and cook for 3–4 min until browned, stirring once throughout.
3 Pick over the chicken carcass, removing all the meat. Discard the bones. Return the meat to the bowl with the stock and vegetables and stir in the watercress and milk. Cover and cook for 12–15 min, stirring once.
4 Allow to cool slightly, remove the bay leaf, then purée the soup in a blender or food processor. The thickness of the soup will depend on the amount of meat from the chicken carcass.
5 Pour the soup into a serving dish. Adjust the seasoning and stir in the soured cream.
6 Reheat the soup for 3–4 min until hot but not boiling, and sprinkle the browned almonds over the top before serving.

Lentil and ham soup *(serves 4–6)*

POWER LEVEL: 100% (FULL)

1 Cook the onion, celery and carrot in a large covered dish for 6–8 min, stirring once.
2 Add the lentils, stock and seasoning. Add the bay leaf, cover and cook for 15–20 min until the lentils are tender and have thickened the soup.
3 Stir in the ham and continue to cook for a further 2–3 min. Adjust the seasoning, stir in the parsley and serve hot.

1 large onion, chopped
2 sticks celery, sliced
1 large carrot, chopped
100g (4oz) lentils
825ml (1½pt) boiling vegetable stock
salt and pepper
1 bay leaf
100g (4oz) cooked ham, diced
1 × 15ml tbsp (1tbsp) chopped parsley

Bean and courgette soup *(serves 6)*

POWER LEVEL: 100% (FULL) AND 50%

1 Place the beans in a bowl and cover with boiling water. Cover the bowl with a lid or pierced clingfilm and heat for 5 min. Leave to stand for 1 hr.
2 Drain the beans, cover with fresh boiling water, cover the bowl and cook for 10 min on 100% (full) and a further 15–20 min on 50% setting until the beans are tender. Leave to stand.
3 Cook the leek in a large, covered casserole dish for 3 min. Add the courgettes, cover and cook for 5 min. Add the stock, herbs and seasoning, cover and cook for 10 min.
4 Stir the mashed potato into the soup and purée in a blender or food processor. Pour the soup into a serving dish or tureen and stir in the drained beans.
5 Cover and reheat for 3–4 min. Adjust the seasoning and stir in the soured cream just before serving.

100g (4oz) flageolet or haricot beans
boiling water
1 leek, finely sliced
450g (1lb) courgettes, trimmed and sliced
825ml (1½pt) boiling vegetable stock
1 × 15ml tbsp (1tbsp) chopped chives
1 × 5ml tsp (1tsp) dill weed
salt and pepper
100g (4oz) cooked potato, creamed or mashed
1 × 15ml tbsp (1tbsp) soured cream

Tomato soup *(serves 4–6)*   *colour page 55*

POWER LEVEL: 100% (FULL)

1 Place the onion, garlic, carrot, celery and bacon in a large covered bowl or dish and cook for 5–6 min, stirring once throughout.
2 Add the tomatoes, stock, tomato paste, salt and pepper and herbs. Mix well, cover and cook for 10–15 min. Remove the bay leaf.
3 Allow the soup to cool slightly then purée in a blender or food processor.
4 Rub the soup through a sieve to remove the tomato skin and seeds, season and add the sugar. Reheat for 2–3 min, and sprinkle with the chopped parsley or oregano before serving.

1 large onion, chopped
1 clove garlic, crushed
1 carrot, diced
2 sticks celery, chopped
4 rashers bacon, de-rinded and chopped
675g (1½lb) tomatoes, roughly chopped
825ml (1½pt) boiling vegetable stock
2 × 15ml tbsp (2tbsp) tomato paste
salt and pepper
1 × 5ml tsp (1tsp) dried oregano
1 bay leaf
1 × 15ml tbsp (1tbsp) dark demerara sugar
for garnish: chopped parsley or oregano

21

1.1 litre (2pt) boiling water
350g (12oz) vegetables and
   peelings
salt and freshly ground black
   pepper
bay leaf
blade mace
4 cloves
1 × 15ml tbsp (1tbsp) chopped
   mixed herbs

Vegetable stock *(makes about 825ml/1¹/₂pt)*
POWER LEVEL: 100% (FULL) AND 50%

1   Pour the water into a large bowl or dish and add the mixture of vegetables
    and peelings, eg onion and skin, carrot, root vegetable peelings, tomato.
2   Add salt, pepper, bay leaf and mace. Cover and cook for 10 min on 100%
    (full) and a further 10–15 min on 50% setting.
3   Strain the stock and add the chopped herbs and extra seasoning if
    necessary.
4   Use immediately or cool and store in the refrigerator for 24 hr, or freeze
    until required.

2 × 15ml tbsp (2tbsp) light
   demerara sugar
salt and pepper
¹/₂ × 5ml tsp (¹/₂tsp) dry
   mustard powder
1 × 15ml tbsp (1tbsp) wine
   vinegar
2 × 15ml tbsp (2tbsp) soured
   cream

Salad dressing *(serves about 6)*

1   Mix together the sugar, salt and pepper and mustard in a small jug. Add
    the vinegar and blend well.
2   Whisk in the soured cream, a little at a time. Chill in the refrigerator and
    stir again before serving.

DO NOT FREEZE

2 egg yolks
¹/₂–1 × 5ml tsp (¹/₂–1tsp) dry
   mustard powder
salt and pepper
2 × 15ml tbsp (2tbsp) vinegar
   or lemon juice
275ml (¹/₂pt) olive or sunflower
   oil
¹/₂ × 5ml tsp (¹/₂tsp) light
   muscovado sugar, optional

Mayonnaise *(makes about 275ml/¹/₂pt)*   *colour opposite*

1   Blend the egg yolks, mustard, salt and pepper, vinegar or lemon juice.
2   Slowly add the oil in a steady stream, whisking constantly until the
    mixture is thick.
3   Taste and add the sugar if required. Store in the refrigerator until needed.

Variations
Garlic: add 1–2 cloves of crushed garlic to taste
Herb: add 1–2 × 15ml tbsp (1–2tbsp) chopped fresh herbs
Tomato: add 1 × 15ml tbsp (1tbsp) tomato paste

Note: *Mayonnaise can be made easily and quickly in a blender or food processor.
Place the egg yolks, mustard, seasoning and vinegar in the goblet and process on
full speed until blended. Pour the oil in a steady stream through the hole in the lid
whilst the blender is running, until the mixture has thickened. Stir in the sugar and
any other flavouring to taste.*

DO NOT FREEZE

1 × 15ml tbsp (1tbsp) olive or
   sunflower oil
1 × 15ml tbsp (1tbsp) finely
   chopped onion
salt and freshly ground black
   pepper
275ml (¹/₂pt) boiling vegetable
   stock
1 × 15ml tbsp (1tbsp) chopped
   fresh herbs of choice
40–50g (1¹/₂–2oz) cooked
   potato, creamed or mashed
1 × 15ml tbsp (2tbsp) soured
   cream

Fresh herb sauce *(makes about 275ml/¹/₂pt)*   *colour opposite*
POWER LEVEL: 100% (FULL)

1   Heat the oil in a bowl for 1 min, add the onion, cover and cook for 2 min.
2   Add the salt and freshly ground black pepper, stock and herbs. Heat
    until boiling, stirring once throughout.
3   Leave to cool slightly and purée in a blender or food processor. Add the
    potato a little at a time until the required consistency is reached.
4   Add the cream to the sauce and adjust the seasoning. Pour into a sauce
    boat or jug and, just before serving, reheat for 1–2 min without boiling.

*Summer Sunset Trifle (page 104); Fresh Herb Sauce (above) with Roast Lamb (page 56);
Pasta Salad (page 90); Mayonnaise (above)*

1 green chilli
½ aubergine
1 large onion
1 courgette
2 cloves garlic, crushed
salt and pepper
1-2 × 5ml tsp (1-2tsp) curry
  powder, to taste
½ × 5ml tsp (½tsp) each
  turmeric and chilli powder
450g (1lb) tomatoes, skinned
  and chopped
2 × 15ml tbsp (2tbsp) tomato
  paste

Curry sauce *(makes about 700ml/1¼pt)*
POWER LEVEL: 100% (FULL)

1 Trim the vegetables and cut into dice. Place in a large covered dish with the garlic, seasoning and spices. Cook for 8–10 min until the vegetables are tender, stirring once or twice throughout.
2 Add the tomatoes and tomato paste and mix well. Cook, uncovered, for 10–12 min until the sauce is thick and the vegetables well blended. Stir once or twice during cooking.
3 Adjust the seasoning before serving hot.

2 egg yolks
25g (1oz) light muscovado
  sugar
1 × 5ml tsp (1tsp) arrowroot
275ml (½pt) milk

Egg custard sauce *(makes about 275ml/½pt)*
POWER LEVEL: 100% (FULL) AND 50%

It is important to cook this sauce on a low power setting otherwise it may curdle

1 Place the egg yolks in a bowl with the sugar and mix well together.
2 Blend the arrowroot with a little of the milk, gradually add the rest stirring continuously.
3 Cook for 2–3 min until slightly thickened, stirring every minute. Pour onto the egg-yolk mixture, stirring well.
4 Reduce to 50% setting and heat for 4–5 min, stirring every minute. Do not allow to boil. Serve hot or cold.

DO NOT FREEZE

25g (1oz) butter, or sunflower
  margarine
25g (1oz) wholewheat flour
275ml (½pt) milk
salt and pepper

White sauce *(makes about 275ml/½pt)*
POWER LEVEL: 100% (FULL)

1 Melt the butter or margarine in a medium-size glass bowl for 1–1½ min. Blend in the flour and gradually stir in the milk.
2 Add the seasonings and cook for 4–5 min, stirring every minute.

Prawn sauce: 100g (4oz) peeled
  prawns
Cheese sauce: 50–75g (2–3oz)
  farmhouse cheddar cheese,
  grated
Mushroom sauce: 50g (2oz)
  mushrooms, chopped
Onion sauce: 100g (4oz) cooked
  onion, chopped
Parsley sauce: 2 × 5ml tsp (2tsp)
  chopped parsley
Egg sauce: 1 hard-boiled egg,
  finely chopped

Variations
Traditional white sauces made with wholewheat flour have a speckled appearance and a delicious nutty flavour. One of the ingredients on the left may be added to the sauce 2 min before the end of the cooking time:

White wine sauce
Follow the recipe, substituting a wine glass of dry white wine for the same amount of milk.

Quick white sauce
Place all the ingredients in a bowl or serving jug and stir briskly. The ingredients will not combine at this stage. Heat for 3–4 min until cooked and thickened, stirring every 15 sec.

Velouté sauce
Follow the recipe for white sauce, replacing the milk with the same quantity of light chicken or fish stock. When cooked, stir in 2 × 15ml tbsp (2tbsp) soured cream.

Tomato sauce *(makes about 275ml/¹/2pt)*
POWER LEVEL: 100% (FULL)

1 Place olive oil, onion and garlic in a bowl and toss well. Cook for 4–5 min until soft. Add all the remaining ingredients and mix well.
2 Cook, uncovered, until soft and the liquid quantity has reduced giving a fairly thick sauce, stirring every 3 min.
3 Use when referred to in recipes or where a good, well-flavoured tomato sauce is required.

1 × 15ml tbsp (1tbsp) olive oil
1 large onion, finely chopped
1–2 cloves garlic, crushed or finely chopped
450g (1lb) tomatoes, skinned and roughly chopped
1 × 15ml tbsp (1tbsp) tomato paste
1 wine glass red wine
few sprigs fresh herbs or 1 × 5ml tsp (1tsp) dried herbs, eg basil
salt and freshly ground black pepper

Meat or poultry gravy *(makes about 275ml/¹/2pt)*
POWER LEVEL: 100% (FULL)

1 Drain any fat from the roasting tray, but keep the meat sediment.
2 Stir in the stock, salt and pepper. Cook for 3–4 min, stirring every minute until boiling vigorously.
3 Pour into a gravy boat or jug and serve hot.

Thin gravy
meat sediment from the roast
275ml (½pt) boiling vegetable stock
salt and pepper

1 Reserve the meat sediment and 2 × 15ml tbsp (2tbsp) meat fat in the roasting dish. Drain off the extra fat.
2 If the fat is starting to solidify, heat in the microwave for 30–60 sec. Stir in the flour and gradually add the stock.
3 Cook for 4–5 min, stirring every minute, until thickened and boiling vigorously. Season to taste.
4 Pour into a gravy boat or jug and serve hot.

Note: *Microwave roasting dishes are available with trivets which allow the juices and fat from the meat to be retained in the dish below*

Thick gravy
meat sediment from the roast
2 × 15ml tbsp (2tbsp) meat-fat residue
1 × 15ml tbsp (1tbsp) wholewheat flour
275ml (½pt) boiling vegetable stock
salt and pepper

Bread sauce *(makes about 825ml/1¹/2pt)*
POWER LEVEL: 100% (FULL)

1 Place the onion in a large covered dish and cook for 5–6 min until tender, stirring once throughout.
2 Spread the bread slices with margarine or butter and cut into small pieces.
3 Add the bread to the onion with salt and pepper and the milk. Cover and cook for 5 min until the bread is soft and has absorbed most of the milk.
4 Mash the sauce with a potato masher. This will give a textured sauce. If a smooth sauce is required, purée the mixture.
5 Season and stir in the soured cream. Reheat for 2–3 min before serving.

1 large onion, chopped
6 slices wholewheat bread, weighing about 175g (6oz)
sunflower margarine or butter
salt and pepper
550ml (1pt) milk
150ml (¼pt) soured cream

Fruit sauce *(makes about 275ml/¹/2pt)*   *colour page 55*
POWER LEVEL: 100% (FULL)

1 Cook the prepared fruit with the liquid in a covered dish for about 6 min or until the fruit is soft.
2 Add sugar to taste and a small knob of butter or margarine to give the sauce a glossy appearance. Serve hot or cold, as it is or puréed.

450g (1lb) prepared fruit eg raspberries, blackberries, gooseberries, sliced apples
2–3 × 15ml tbsp (2–3tbsp) water or wine
sugar to taste
small knob butter or sunflower margarine

Snacks and Meals-in-one

Many recipes throughout the book can be served as snack or supper dishes, but the selection here includes a variety of recipes for your guidance. Most of the dishes use simple ingredients, are quick to prepare and provide a perfect answer when there is not time to cook a full-scale meal or when you just don't feel like eating one!

225g (8oz) kipper fillets
100g (4oz) mushrooms, sliced
2 courgettes, sliced
4 eggs, beaten
pepper and salt
25–50g (1–2oz) wholewheat
   breadcrumbs
for garnish: tomato slices

Kipper and vegetable bake *(serves 2–3)* *colour opposite*
POWER LEVEL: 100% (FULL)

1 Cook the kippers on a plate or in a shallow dish, covered with pierced clingfilm, for 3–4 min. Stand for a few minutes, then skin and flake the fillets.
2 In a 20cm (8in) oval or round dish, cook the mushrooms and courgettes, covered, for 5–6 min, stirring once during cooking. Stir in the flaked kippers.
3 Beat the eggs with some pepper, adding salt only if necessary. Pour the eggs over the fish and vegetables. Cook for 4–5 min or until set, stirring after 2 min.
4 Sprinkle with the breadcrumbs and heat for a further 1–1½ min. Garnish with the tomato slices before serving hot.

DO NOT FREEZE

1 × 15ml tbsp (1tbsp)
   sunflower oil
2 bacon rashers, de-rinded and
   chopped
1 medium onion, chopped
2 sticks celery, chopped
350g (12oz) potatoes, cut into
   small dice
350g (12oz) white fish fillets,
   cut into 2·5cm (1in) pieces
550ml (1pt) boiling vegetable
   stock
¼ × 5ml tsp (¼tsp) turmeric
¼ × 5ml tsp (¼tsp) dried
   thyme
1 bay leaf
salt and freshly ground black
   pepper
225g (8oz) shellfish, ie cockles,
   mussels or peeled prawns
150ml (¼pt) soured cream or
   yoghurt
2 × 15ml tbsp (2tbsp) chopped
   parsley
for serving: wholewheat bread or
   toast

Fish chowder *(serves 4)* *colour opposite*
POWER LEVEL: 100% (FULL)

1 Mix together the oil, bacon, onion and celery in a large casserole dish, cover and cook for 2 min.
2 Add the potatoes, mix well together, cover and cook for 11–12 min, stirring twice throughout.
3 Add the fish, stock, turmeric, thyme, bay leaf and seasoning. Cover and cook for 5–6 min.
4 Adjust the seasoning and add the shellfish. Cover and heat through for 2 min.
5 Stir in the soured cream or yoghurt and 1 × 15ml tbsp (1tbsp) chopped parsley. Sprinkle with the remaining parsley and serve hot with wholewheat bread or toast.

Fish Chowder (above); Bananas and Bacon on Toast (page 28); Kipper and Vegetable Bake (above)

4 rashers bacon, de-rinded
and chopped
2 slices wholewheat toast,
buttered or spread with
sunflower margarine
2 small bananas, thinly sliced
for garnish: chopped parsley

Bananas and bacon on toast *(serves 2)*   *colour page 27*
POWER LEVEL: 100% (FULL)

1 Cook the bacon in a small dish, covered with kitchen paper, for 3–4 min.
2 Place the prepared toast on a serving plate or individual plates. Arrange the banana slices on the toast and top with the bacon.
3 Heat, uncovered, for 2½–3 min until hot through. Garnish with chopped parsley before serving.

DO NOT FREEZE

1 large onion, chopped
225g (8oz) smoked streaky
bacon, de-rinded and cut into
strips
225g (8oz) lentils
3 × 15ml tbsp (3tbsp) tomato
paste
825ml (1½pt) boiling chicken
stock
salt and freshly ground black
pepper
for serving: crusty bread or salad

Lentils with bacon *(serves 4)*
POWER LEVEL: 100% (FULL)

1 Place the onion in a large casserole dish, cover and cook for 2 min. Add the bacon and cook for a further 4 min, stirring once throughout.
2 Add the lentils, tomato paste and boiling stock and mix well. Cover with a lid or pierced clingfilm and cook for 20–25 min until the lentils are tender. The consistency should be quite thick—if necessary cook, uncovered, for a further 3–5 min to reduce the liquid slightly. Leave to stand for 5 min.
3 Add salt and freshly ground black pepper to taste and serve hot with crusty bread or salad.

25g (1oz) butter or sunflower
margarine
100g (4oz) button mushrooms,
wiped
salt and pepper
2 slices hot toast, spread with
butter or sunflower
margarine

Mushrooms on toast *(serves 1–2)*
POWER LEVEL: 100% (FULL)

1 Melt the butter or sunflower margarine in a small bowl for 1 min. Add the mushrooms, salt and pepper, and toss well.
2 Cover and cook for 2–2½ min and drain. Serve hot on the prepared toast.

DO NOT FREEZE

2 large potatoes, weighed
4 kidneys, cored and diced
1 × 15ml tbsp (1tbsp)
wholewheat flour
freshly ground black pepper
and salt
6 × 15ml tbsp (6tbsp) water or
stock
salt
for garnish: natural yoghurt or
soured cream and chopped
chives or spring onion tops

Jacket potatoes stuffed with kidneys *(serves 2)*
POWER LEVEL: 100% (FULL)

1 Scrub and score the potatoes with a cross on the top. Place on kitchen paper and cook at 100% (full) allowing 10–12 min per 450g (1lb). Leave to stand.
2 Toss the kidneys in the flour and place in a small dish, adding plenty of freshly ground black pepper. Cover and cook for 5–6 min, stirring once during cooking.
3 Add the water or stock, and cook, uncovered, for 3–4 min, stirring every minute until thickened and boiling. Season, adding extra pepper and salt to taste.
4 Cut the potatoes through the cross about 12mm (½in) and carefully open them. Spoon in the kidney filling and reheat, uncovered, for 2–3 min.
5 Spoon yoghurt or soured cream to taste over the potatoes, sprinkle with chopped chives or spring onion tops and serve.

DO NOT FREEZE

Jacket potatoes stuffed with cheese, apple and tuna *(serves 2)*
POWER LEVEL: 100% (FULL)

1 Prepare and cook the potatoes as given on page 28.
2 Cook the onion in a small covered dish for 2–3 min until soft, stirring once. Beat the curd cheese into the onion.
3 Toss the apple in the lemon juice and add to the cheese and onion mixture. Flake the tuna fish and add it to the filling with the chopped mint. Season to taste with salt and paprika.
4 Cut the potatoes through the cross about 12mm (½in) and carefully open them. Pile the filling into the potatoes and reheat, uncovered, for 2–3 min. Serve immediately.

DO NOT FREEZE

2 large potatoes
1 small onion, chopped
100g (4oz) curd cheese
1 red eating apple, cored and diced
lemon juice
90g (3½oz) can tuna fish in brine, drained
sprig fresh mint, chopped
salt and paprika

Cauliflower medley *(serves 4–6)*
POWER LEVEL: 100% (FULL)

1 Place the cauliflower florets in a large casserole dish with the salted water, cover and cook allowing 10–11 min per 450g (1lb). Stir once or twice during cooking then leave to stand, covered.
2 Place the onion in a small bowl, cover and cook for 3 min. Add the flaked tuna, yoghurt and 1 × 15ml tbsp (1tbsp) chopped chives. Season to taste with salt and pepper and heat, covered, for 3 min, stirring once throughout.
3 Drain the water from the cauliflower. Add the tuna fish mixture, pine nuts and mix well together. Sprinkle the dish with the grated cheese mixed with the remaining chopped chives and heat for 2–3 min until the cheese has melted, or brown under a hot grill.

1 large cauliflower, cut into large florets
2–3 × 15ml tbsp (2–3tbsp) salted water
1 onion, finely chopped
1 × 200g (7oz) can tuna in brine, drained and flaked
150ml (¼pt) natural yoghurt
2 × 15ml tbsp (2tbsp) chopped chives
salt and pepper
50g (2oz) pine nuts
50g (2oz) farmhouse cheddar cheese, grated

Left-over beef cobbler *(serves 4–6)*
POWER LEVEL: 100% (FULL)

1 Cook the onion, leek and parsnip in a large covered casserole dish for 8–10 min until tender, stirring once during cooking.
2 Add the beef, boiling stock, tomato paste and salt and pepper. Stir well, cover and cook for 5 min.
3 Place the flour, baking powder, mustard and pinch salt in a bowl and rub in the butter or margarine until the mixture resembles fine breadcrumbs. Stir in 50g (2oz) of the cheese and mix the ingredients to a soft scone dough using milk or water to mix.
4 Lightly knead the dough and roll out on a floured surface to a circle slightly smaller than the casserole dish. Cut into 6–8 triangles or wedges and arrange them on top of the casserole with the thin ends towards the centre of the dish.
5 Cook, uncovered, for 5–6 min until the scones are risen and cooked through. Mix the remaining cheese with the chopped parsley and sprinkle over the top before serving hot.

1 large onion, chopped
1 leek, trimmed and sliced
1 parsnip, diced
350g (12oz) cooked beef, minced or chopped
425ml (¾pt) boiling vegetable stock
2 × 15ml tbsp (2tbsp) tomato paste
salt and pepper
175g (6oz) wholewheat flour
2 × 5ml tsp (2tsp) baking powder
½ × 5ml tsp (½tsp) mustard powder
pinch salt
40g (1½oz) butter or vegetable margarine
75g (3oz) farmhouse cheddar cheese, grated
milk or water to mix
chopped parsley

2 onions, chopped
1 red pepper
1 green pepper
25g (1oz) wholewheat flour
275ml (½pt) boiling vegetable
    stock
450g (1lb) cooked pork, diced
salt and pepper
½ × 5ml tsp (½tsp) paprika
2 × 15ml tbsp (2tbsp) yoghurt
    or soured cream
for garnish: paprika
for serving: crisp lettuce or a
    green salad

Peppered pork pot *(serves 4–5)*   *colour opposite*
POWER LEVEL: 100% (FULL)

This is an impressive dish, quick to prepare using left-over cooked meat, and makes a substantial supper dish

1   Place the onion in a large casserole dish. Deseed the peppers and cut them into thin 5cm (2in) strips. Add them to the dish and cook, covered, for 5–6 min, stirring once throughout.
2   Stir the flour into the vegetables, gradually add the stock mixing well together. Cook, uncovered, for 4–5 min until boiling, stirring every minute.
3   Add the diced pork, salt and pepper to taste and the paprika. Cover the dish and heat for 5–6 min.
4   Stir in the yoghurt or soured cream and check the seasoning. Sprinkle with paprika to garnish and serve with crisp lettuce or a green salad.

1 onion, chopped
1 clove garlic, crushed
1 aubergine, halved lengthways
    and sliced
1 courgette, sliced
1–2 × 5ml tsp (1–2tsp) curry
    powder, to taste
4 tomatoes, skinned and
    chopped
150ml (¼pt) boiling vegetable
    stock or water
salt
4 hard-boiled eggs, peeled
1 large banana, sliced
lemon juice
for serving: boiled rice (page 77)
    or wholewheat toast and
    natural yoghurt

Quick curried eggs *(serves 4)*   *colour opposite*
POWER LEVEL: 100% (FULL)

1   Place the onion, garlic, aubergine and courgette in a casserole dish and mix with the curry powder. Cover and cook for 8–10 min, stirring once throughout.
2   Add the tomatoes, stock and a little salt. Cover and cook for a further 5 min.
3   Place the hard-boiled eggs in the curry and heat through, covered, for 3–4 min. Adjust the seasoning.
4   Brush the slices of banana with lemon juice and arrange them around the edge of the dish.
5   Serve with boiled rice or wholewheat toast and natural yoghurt.

DO NOT FREEZE

675g (1½lb) raw mixed
    vegetables, ie onion, carrot,
    parsnip, leek, celery etc
salt and pepper
2 × 15ml tbsp (2tbsp) water
1 × 15ml tbsp (1tbsp) chopped
    fresh herbs or 1 × 5ml tsp
    (1tsp) dried herbs
50g (2oz) peanuts
100g (4oz) medium oatmeal
50g (2oz) bran
50g (2oz) butter or vegetable
    margarine
50g (2oz) farmhouse cheddar
    cheese
1 × 15ml tbsp (1tbsp) chopped
    parsley
for garnish: tomato slices

Vegetarian cheese crumble *(serves 4)*   *colour opposite*
POWER LEVEL: 100% (FULL)

1   Prepare the vegetables, slicing or chopping them. Place in a casserole dish with a little salt, the water and the herbs.
2   Cover and cook for 10–12 min or until tender, stirring once during cooking. Drain off any excess water and add the peanuts.
3   Mix together the oatmeal and bran. Rub in the butter or margarine until the mixture resembles breadcrumbs. Stir in the cheese, parsley, and a little salt and pepper.
4   Sprinkle the crumble over the vegetables in the casserole dish. Cook, uncovered, for 8–10 min or until the crumble is slightly firm.
5   Garnish with tomato slices before serving.

Vegetarian Cheese Crumble (above); Peppered Pork Pot (above); Quick Curried Eggs (above)

900g (2lb) fresh spinach
salt and pepper
2 eggs, beaten
100g (4oz) cheddar cheese,
  grated
275ml (½pt) natural yoghurt
for serving: fresh wholewheat
  toast, buttered or spread
  with sunflower margarine

Spinach au gratin *(serves 3)*
POWER LEVEL: 100% (FULL) AND 60%

The dish is browned under a hot grill before serving

1 Wash the spinach well and break off the thick stalks. Shake it dry and place in a large covered dish. Cook for 9–12 min, stirring once during cooking.
2 Drain the spinach well in a colander and chop with a metal spoon while squeezing out the water. Season well with salt and pepper and arrange in the bottom of a shallow serving dish.
3 Beat the eggs with 75g (3oz) of the grated cheese and add the natural yoghurt, mixing well together. Pour the mixture over the spinach.
4 Cook, uncovered, for 10–12 min on 60% setting or until the topping has set. Meanwhile, cook the toast under a hot grill.
5 When the gratin topping is set, sprinkle it with the remaining cheese and brown under the hot grill before serving with the toast.

DO NOT FREEZE

1 large onion, chopped
1 clove garlic, crushed
4 tomatoes, skinned and
  chopped
175g (6oz) mushrooms, sliced
1 bay leaf
salt and pepper
275ml (½pt) boiling vegetable
  stock
2 × 15ml tbsp (2tbsp) tomato
  paste
175g (6oz) wholewheat flour
2 × 5ml tsp (2tsp) baking
  powder
pinch salt
50g (2oz) suet, grated
50g (2oz) farmhouse cheddar
  cheese, grated
water to mix
for garnish: few sliced
  mushrooms

Cheese dumplings with mushroom sauce *(serves 3–4)*
POWER LEVEL: 100% (FULL)

1 Place the onion, garlic and tomatoes in a large casserole dish, cover and cook for 5 min, stirring once during cooking.
2 Add the mushrooms, bay leaf and seasoning, stir in the stock and tomato paste. Cook, uncovered, for about 10 min, stirring once or twice, until the sauce has reduced slightly.
3 Place the flour, baking powder, pinch salt, suet and cheese in a bowl and add enough water to mix to a workable dough. Knead lightly on a floured board and divide into 6–8 dumplings.
4 Add the dumplings to the sauce, cover and cook for 5–7 min until risen and cooked through. Garnish with a few mushroom slices before serving hot.

Baked stuffed grapefruits *(serves 4)*
POWER LEVEL: 100% (FULL)

1 Cut the top from each grapefruit and cut round the flesh with a serrated knife. Scoop out the fruit, remove the pips and chop the flesh.
2 Place the grapefruit flesh in a bowl with the onion and peppers and cook, covered, for 5 min, stirring once during cooking.
3 Add all the remaining ingredients except the lettuce and stir well. Cook, uncovered, for 8–10 min or until the grapefruit juice has reduced.
4 Pile the filling into the grapefruit shells, garnish with the tops from the fruits and serve on a bed of lettuce.

DO NOT FREEZE

4 small grapefruit
1 onion, chopped
½ red pepper, deseeded and finely diced
½ green pepper, deseeded and finely diced
75g (3oz) cooked long-grain brown rice (page 77)
50g (2oz) raisins
100g (4oz) cooked chicken, chopped
1 × 15ml tbsp (1tbsp) freshly chopped tarragon
salt and pepper
for serving: lettuce

Special omelette *(serves 3–4)*
POWER LEVEL: 100% (FULL) AND 50%

1 Place the noodles in a large bowl or dish and add sufficient boiling water to cover. Add salt to taste, cover and cook for 3 min on 100% (full) and leave to stand for 5 min. Drain well.
2 Melt the butter or margarine for 1½–2 min in a 20–22·5 cm (8–9in) round dish until bubbling. Stir in the mushrooms and peas, cover and cook for 4 min.
3 Add the prawns and noodles and mix well. Continue to cook for 2 min, stirring once halfway through.
4 Heat the milk or water for 1–1½ min until boiling and beat into the eggs with salt and pepper.
5 Pour the eggs quickly over the hot noodle mixture and stir. Reduce to 50% setting, cover and cook for 9–10 min. Sprinkle with the cheese and continue to cook, uncovered, for a further 1½–2 min.
6 Stand for 3 min before serving hot in wedges with green salad and wholewheat bread.

DO NOT FREEZE

100g (4oz) chinese egg noodles
275–425ml (½–¾pt) boiling water
salt
50g (2oz) butter or vegetable margarine
100g (4oz) button mushrooms, sliced
225g (8oz) shelled peas
100g (4oz) peeled prawns
6 × 15ml tbsp (6tbsp) milk or water
6 eggs, size 3
pepper
50g (2oz) farmhouse cheddar cheese, grated
for serving: green salad and wholewheat bread

Bubble and squeak *(serves 2)*
POWER LEVEL: 100% (FULL)

This is a good way of using left-over vegetables and is cooked in the browning dish

1 Preheat a large browning dish for 5 min.
2 Mix together the potato and green vegetables and season with salt and pepper.
3 Brush the base of the browning dish with oil. Add the vegetables and press onto the hot surface of the dish using a palette knife or heatproof spatula and forming the vegetables into a large round.
4 Cook for 3 min. Turn the vegetables over, re-form into a round and cook for a further 2–3 min. Serve immediately.

Note: *For a more substantial snack, add 2 beaten eggs to the mixture*

DO NOT FREEZE

350g (12oz) left-over potatoes, mashed or creamed
225g (8oz) left-over cooked green vegetables, ie cabbage, sprouts
salt and pepper
sunflower oil

From the Dairy

Cottage Cheese preparation (page 37); Yoghurt with Cucumber (below); Cottage Cheese and Ham Cocottes (below); Cheese and Apple Toasties (page 36)

Foods from the dairy include butter, cheese, milk, cream and yoghurt. Also included in this section are a few recipes using eggs and some using tofu (a soya bean curd), although neither are strictly dairy products.

Eggs and cheese are both high protein foods and, as such, are sensitive to heat. As cooking is so fast in the microwave, it is advisable to slightly under-cook as egg yolks set more quickly than the whites and cheese tends to become leathery in texture if overcooked. Although many egg and cheese-based dishes can be cooked on 100% (full) setting, lower power levels give the flexibility in control for some recipes to ensure results which are near perfect every time. When cooking eggs in the microwave, don't forget to prick the yolks with a sharp-pointed knife or cocktail stick before cooking, and remove them from the oven just before they are set as they will carry on cooking for a short while afterwards. If they are not set sufficiently for your liking, return them to the microwave for a further 10–15 sec.

Milk heats more quickly than water, although this depends on the starting temperature. Ensure there is enough room in the container for milk to boil if required. Heating times from cold using 100% (full) power setting are 1–1¼ min for 150ml (¼pt), 2–2½ min for 275ml (½pt) and 5–6 min for 550ml (1pt) milk.

Soured cream is made with a culture in a similar way to yoghurt. It has a high fat content but is lighter in texture with a more refreshing flavour than double cream, which is rarely used in wholefood cooking. Natural yoghurt and cottage cheese are popular wholefoods and there are many types available but, best of all, make your own (see page 36).

---

1 small onion, finely chopped
½ cucumber, grated and drained well
1–2 cloves garlic, crushed, optional
425ml (¾pt) natural yoghurt
1 lemon, grated rind
salt and pepper
for garnish: paprika for sprinkling
for serving: see method 3

Yoghurt with cucumber *(serves 4–6)*   *colour opposite*
POWER LEVEL: 100% (FULL)

1 Place the onion in a small covered dish, cook for 2–3 min until tender. Allow to cool.
2 Mix together all the ingredients except the paprika, adding salt and pepper to taste. Turn the mixture into a serving dish and chill before serving sprinkled with paprika.
3 Serve with sticks of carrot and celery and pieces of green or red pepper as a dip, or serve as an accompaniment to hot, spicy dishes or as a light creamy salad. In addition, fresh milk may be stirred in to produce a delicious chilled soup.

225g (8oz) cottage cheese
175g (6oz) cooked ham, diced
2 eggs, beaten
salt and pepper
1 × 15ml tbsp (1tbsp) chopped chives
paprika or chopped parsley
for serving: freshly cooked spinach or a salad

Cottage cheese and ham cocottes *(serves 2–4)*   *colour opposite*
POWER LEVEL: 60%

1 Lightly oil 4 small ramekin dishes.
2 Beat the cottage cheese in a bowl, add the ham and eggs and mix well. Season to taste with salt and pepper and add the chopped chives.
3 Spoon the mixture into the greased ramekin dishes and cook, uncovered, for 8–10 min on 60% setting until set.
4 Sprinkle with paprika or chopped parsley and serve hot with freshly cooked spinach or a salad.

DO NOT FREEZE

3 dessert apples
½ lemon, juice
175g (6oz) farmhouse cheddar
  cheese, grated
1 × 15ml tbsp (1tbsp) natural
  yoghurt
1 × 15ml tbsp (1tbsp) peanut
  butter
1 × 15ml tbsp (1tbsp) chopped
  parsley
salt and pepper
4 slices freshly cooked
  wholewheat toast
for garnish: watercress

Cheese and apple toasties *(serves 4)*   *colour page 35*
POWER LEVEL: 70%

1 Core one of the apples and slice it into 4 rings. Brush the rings with the lemon juice. Grate the remaining two apples.
2 Mix together the grated apples, cheese, yoghurt, peanut butter, parsley and salt and pepper. Spread the mixture on the freshly made toast.
3 Place the toasties onto a serving plate and cook for 3–4 min on 70% setting until the cheese is melted.
4 Garnish each slice with an apple ring and watercress, and serve immediately.

DO NOT FREEZE

550ml (1pt) milk
boiling water
3 × 15ml tbsp (3tbsp) natural
  yoghurt

Natural yoghurt *(makes about 550ml/1pt)*   *colour page 55*
POWER LEVEL: 100% (FULL)

1 Place the milk in a large bowl or jug and heat, uncovered, for 5–6 min or until boiling. Cover and allow the milk to cool until tepid—this may take about 30 min, depending on the room temperature and the type of bowl or jug used.
2 Meanwhile, warm a wide-necked vacuum flask with boiling water. Drain.
3 Stir the yoghurt into the milk and pour into the warmed flask. Seal and leave for 8 hr or overnight, undisturbed, to set.
4 Store in the refrigerator and use as required.

DO NOT FREEZE

50g (2oz) sunflower margarine
150ml (¼pt) water
65g (2½oz) fine wholewheat
  flour
2 eggs, beaten
350g (12oz) cottage cheese,
  sieved
1 orange, grated rind and juice
1–2 × 15ml tbsp (1–2tbsp)
  light muscovado sugar
2 × 5ml tsp (2tsp) arrowroot
150ml (¼pt) water
4 × 15ml tbsp (½tbsp) orange
  marmalade

Cheese and orange choux buns *(serves 4–6)*   *colour page 115*
POWER LEVEL: 100% (FULL)
CONVENTIONAL OVEN TEMPERATURE: 210°C (425°F) MARK 7

1 Grease two baking trays and preheat the conventional oven.
2 Place the margarine and 150ml (¼pt) water in a bowl and heat, uncovered, in the microwave for 5–6 min until boiling rapidly. Quickly add the flour and beat well until the mixture leaves the sides of the bowl. Cool slightly.
3 Gradually add the beaten eggs to the flour, beating well. Place walnut-size spoonfuls of the paste onto the greased baking sheets. Bake in the conventional oven for 20 min.
4 Make a slit in each bun then return them to the oven. Reduce the temperature to 190°C (375°F) mark 5 and cook for a further 10 min. Leave to cool on a wire rack.
5 Beat the cottage cheese with the orange rind and a little of the juice and sweeten to taste with light muscovado sugar. Fill each of the choux buns with the mixture and pile them onto a serving plate.
6 Blend the arrowroot with the 150ml (¼pt) water in a small bowl and add the marmalade and remaining orange juice. Heat for 3–4 min in the microwave, stirring every minute until thickened and boiling.
7 Pour the sauce over the choux buns and serve immediately.

DO NOT FREEZE

Cottage cheese *(makes about 75g/3oz)*   *colour page 35*
POWER LEVEL: 100% (FULL) AND 30%

550ml (1pt) milk
1½ × 15ml tbsp (1½tbsp) rennet
salt and pepper
chopped fresh herbs to taste

1 Heat the milk, uncovered, for 1½–2 min on 100% (full) setting until just tepid. Stir in the rennet and heat for a further 4–5 min on 30% setting until the milk has set.
2 Stir the milk gently, until the curds and whey separate. Pour the mixture into a sieve lined with muslin or a clean J-cloth. Tie the corners of the cloth together and suspend it over a bowl to drain.
3 Leave the cheese overnight, or for 2–3 hr if the cloth is gently squeezed occasionally.
4 Empty the cheese into a bowl and mash it with a fork. Season to taste with the salt and pepper and chopped fresh herbs. Store in the refrigerator and use as required.

DO NOT FREEZE

Yoghurt rice *(serves 3–4)*
POWER LEVEL: 100% (FULL)

225g (8oz) long-grain brown rice
pinch salt
550ml (1pt) boiling vegetable stock
1 green chilli, deseeded and finely chopped
small bunch coriander leaves, finely chopped
small piece root ginger, peeled and grated
1 × 15ml tbsp (1tbsp) sunflower oil
½ × 5ml tsp (½tsp) black mustard seeds
3 dried curry leaves, crushed
pinch asafoetida powder
150ml (¼pt) natural yoghurt
salt and pepper
for garnish: lemon or lime butterflies

1 Place the rice in a bowl with the pinch of salt and boiling stock, stir well, cover and cook for 20–25 min. Leave to stand for 5 min. Stir in the chilli, coriander and ginger.
2 Heat the oil in a small dish for 2½ min, add the mustard seeds and cook for 2½ min. Stir in the curry leaves and asafoetida powder.
3 Add the spices to the rice with the yoghurt and mix well. Reheat if necessary, uncovered, for 1–2 min, and serve garnished with the lemon or lime butterflies.

Note: *Yoghurt rice goes extremely well with tandoori chicken (page 65) and vegetable curries*

DO NOT FREEZE

225g (8oz) farmhouse cheddar
  cheese, grated
2 courgettes or ½ cucumber,
  trimmed and grated
1 clove garlic, crushed
425ml (¾pt) natural yoghurt
1 × 15ml tbsp (1tbsp)
  mayonnaise
½ × 5ml tsp (½tsp) mustard
  powder
1 × 15ml tbsp (1tbsp) chopped
  chives or parsley
½ × 5ml tsp (½tsp) paprika
salt and pepper
6 × 15ml tbsp (6tbsp) white
  wine or water
25g (1oz) or 2 packets gelatin
for garnish: paprika for
  sprinkling and watercress
for serving: wholewheat pitta
  bread or tomato and onion
  salad

Cheddar mousse *(serves 4–8)* *colour opposite*
POWER LEVEL: 100% (FULL)

Serve either as a starter or a main course

1 In a large bowl mix together all the ingredients except the wine and gelatin.
2 Heat the wine in a small bowl or dish for 30 sec, add the gelatin and stir to dissolve. Heat for a further 15–30 sec, without boiling, until the gelatin is completely dissolved. Beat the gelatin into the cheese mixture.
3 Rinse a 17.5cm (7in) ring mould in cold water. Spoon the mousse into the mould and smooth the top. Leave until set.
4 Ease the mousse away from the sides of the mould with your finger-tips and invert onto a serving plate. Garnish with a little sprinkled paprika and watercress.
5 Serve with wholewheat pitta-bread fingers or tomato and onion salad.

DO NOT FREEZE

75g (3oz) sunflower margarine
175g (6oz) muesli, finely
  ground
1 × 15ml tbsp (1tbsp) light
  muscovado sugar
450g (1lb) cooking apples,
  sliced
1 lemon, grated rind and juice
sugar or honey to taste
1 × 5ml tsp (1tsp) mixed spice
150g (5oz) tofu, cut into cubes
2 eggs, beaten
for decoration: dark demerara
  sugar

Baked tofu apple flan *(serves 6–8)*
POWER LEVEL: 100% (FULL) AND 60%

1 Melt the margarine in a 20cm (8in) flan dish for 1½–2 min, stir in the muesli and muscovado sugar. Press the mixture into the bottom of the dish using the back of a spoon.
2 Place the apple slices in a bowl or dish with the lemon rind and juice. Cover and cook for 6–7 min, stirring once during cooking. Sweeten to taste with sugar or honey and allow to cool.
3 Place the cooled apple, mixed spice and tofu in a blender or food processor and purée until creamy. Add the beaten eggs and mix well.
4 Pour the filling over the prepared base and cook, uncovered, on 60% setting for 12–15 min or until set. Whilst the flan is still hot, sprinkle with dark demerara sugar.
5 Chill in the refrigerator before serving.

DO NOT FREEZE

275ml (½pt) milk
150ml (¼pt) soured cream
3 eggs, lightly beaten
2 × 15ml tbsp (2tbsp)
  muscovado sugar
grated nutmeg for sprinkling

*Cheddar Mousse (above); Egg
Custard Creams (above); Trout with
Grapefruit and Cashews (page 50)*

Egg custard creams *(serves 4–5)* *colour opposite*
POWER LEVEL: 100% (FULL) AND 50%

1 Heat the milk in a measuring jug or bowl for 3 min on 100% (full) setting. Add the cream, eggs and sugar and whisk lightly.
2 Strain and pour the mixture into individual bowls or ramekin dishes. Sprinkle with nutmeg.
3 Arrange in a circle in the microwave and cook on 50% setting for 10–12 min, turning the dishes if necessary halfway through.
4 Serve warm, or chill in the refrigerator.

DO NOT FREEZE

a little butter or sunflower
    margarine
2 eggs

Baked eggs *(serves 1–2)*
POWER LEVEL: 50%

Baked eggs may be used as hard-boiled eggs when required chopped for salads or fillings

1 Lightly grease 2 small dishes or bowls with the butter or margarine. Break the eggs into the dishes and prick the yolks.
2 Cover and cook for 2–2½ min, turning the dishes if necessary, halfway through.

DO NOT FREEZE

---

1 × 15ml tbsp (1tbsp)
    sunflower oil
½ × 5ml tsp (½tsp) cumin
    seeds
a few dried curry leaves,
    crushed
pinch turmeric
pinch asafoetida powder
275ml (½pt) natural yoghurt
550ml (1pt) water
salt to taste

Indian yoghurt drink *(serves 4)*   *colour page 87*
POWER LEVEL: 100% (FULL)

1 Heat the oil in a small dish for 2½ min. Add the cumin seeds and curry leaves and cook for 3 min. Stir in the turmeric and asafoetida powder.
2 Whisk together the yoghurt and water, add the spices and salt to taste. Serve immediately.

DO NOT FREEZE

15g (½oz) butter
3 eggs, separated
2 × 15ml tbsp (2tbsp) milk
salt and pepper

Soufflé omelette *(serves 1–2)*
POWER LEVEL: 100% (FULL) AND 30%

1 Melt the butter in a 20cm (8in) round, shallow dish for 30 sec.
2 Whisk the egg yolks, milk and seasoning together. In a separate bowl, whisk the egg white until stiff.
3 Carefully fold the egg whites into the egg-yolk mixture. Turn into the prepared dish, smooth the mixture over the dish.
4 Cook, uncovered, on 30% setting for 5–6 min until the centre of the omelette is set. Fill as required and serve hot, folded in half. The top of the omelette may be browned under a hot grill if required.

DO NOT FREEZE

---

1 small onion, finely chopped
1 green pepper, deseeded and
    finely chopped
1 clove garlic, crushed
100g (4oz) mushrooms, finely
    chopped
100g (4oz) farmhouse cheddar
    cheese, finely grated
225g (8oz) curd cheese or
    sieved cottage cheese
1 × 15ml tbsp (1tbsp) tomato
    paste
salt and freshly ground black
    pepper

Cheese and vegetable dip *(serves 6–8)*   *colour page 7*
POWER LEVEL: 100% (FULL)

1 Cook the onion, green pepper and garlic in a small covered dish for 3–4 min, stirring once during cooking. Add the mushrooms and cook for a further 3–4 min.
2 Stir the grated cheddar into the hot vegetables until the cheese has softened, allow to cool.
3 Add the curd or cottage cheese, tomato paste and seasoning to taste. Mix well together.
4 Place the mixture in a serving dish and chill in the refrigerator. Use as a dip or for sandwich fillings.

DO NOT FREEZE

Cheese and spinach tart *(serves 4)*
POWER LEVEL: 100% (FULL) AND 50%

1 Place the flour and pinch of salt in a bowl, rub in the butter or vegetable margarine until the mixture resembles breadcrumbs. Add sufficient tepid water to mix to a manageable dough, knead lightly and roll out to line a 17.5–20cm (7–8in) flan dish.
2 Line the sides of the pastry flan with small pieces of aluminium foil and prick the base with a fork. Line with kitchen paper towel and fill with baking beans. Cook for 4 min, remove the baking beans, paper and foil, and cook for a further 1½–2 min.
3 Place the onion in a small dish, cover with pierced clingfilm or a lid and cook for 2 min.
4 Cream the cheese until soft, then add the egg yolks, beating well together. Stir in the onion, spinach and salt and pepper to taste. Spoon the mixture into the pastry case.
5 Reduce to 50% setting and cook the flan for 12–14 min until the filling is set. Serve hot or cold.

175g (6oz) wholewheat flour
pinch salt
75g (3oz) butter or vegetable margarine
tepid water to mix
1 small onion, chopped
225g (8oz) curd cheese
2 egg yolks
225g (8oz) cooked spinach, chopped
salt and pepper

Cheese potato pie *(serves 2–4)*
POWER LEVEL: 100% (FULL)

Serve as a vegetable with a main coarse, or on its own as a snack

1 Slice the potatoes very thinly using a vegetable slicer, or pare with a vegetable peeler. Rinse well in cold water.
2 Place the potato slices in a bowl, sprinkle with salt and just cover with boiling water. Heat in the microwave until the potatoes are transparent and soft. Drain well.
3 Arrange overlapping layer of potatoes in the bottom of a lightly greased dish, sprinkle with some of the cheese, onion and seasoning and dot with butter or vegetable margarine. Continue the layers, alternating the potatoes with the cheese and onion, finishing with a layer of cheese.
4 Cover and cook for 6–8 min, uncovered. Sprinkle with paprika and serve hot.

450g (1lb) potatoes, peeled
2 × 5ml tsp (2tsp) salt
boiling water
175g (6oz) cheese, grated
1 small onion, grated
salt and freshly ground black pepper
25g (1oz) butter or vegetable margarine
paprika for sprinkling

Spiced aubergine dip *(serves 6–8)*   *colour page 87*
POWER LEVEL: 100% (FULL)

1 Heat the oil in a large dish for 2 min. Add all the vegetables and spices, stir, cover and cook for 12–15 min until the vegetables are tender, stirring well once or twice during cooking. Allow to cool.
2 Place the vegetables in a blender or food processor with the tofu and yoghurt. Purée until smooth, adding a little extra yoghurt if necessary to give a creamy consistency. Adjust the seasoning.
3 Turn the dip into a serving dish and chill well. Garnish with a little grated carrot before serving.

1 × 15ml tbsp (1tbsp) sunflower or olive oil
1 onion, finely chopped
1–2 cloves garlic, crushed
1 red pepper, deseeded and chopped
1 medium aubergine, trimmed and diced
salt and freshly ground black pepper
1 × 5ml tsp (1tsp) each ground cumin and ginger
pinch cayenne pepper
150g (5oz) tofu, cut into cubes
3–4 × 15ml tbsp (3–4tbsp) natural yoghurt
for garnish: grated carrot

Fish and Shellfish

Moules Marinière (page 45);
Scallops with Avocado Dressing
(below)

Probably more than most other foods, fish benefits from being cooked by microwave as the moist textures and delicate flavours are preserved and to a degree even enhanced by this cooking method. Whichever variety of fresh fish you select from your local fishmonger—a delicate white fish, a richer oily fish or one or more of the delicious types of shellfish—all are available to the wholefood cook, providing a good source of protein whether served as a starter, a main course, or light lunch or supper dish. The traditional deep-fried fish and chips, rich in fat or oil, cannot be classed as a wholefood meal and, in fact, deep frying must not be attempted in the microwave as the temperature of the oil cannot be controlled.

Fish which are normally steamed, poached or baked are particularly good for the wholefood microwave cook. Whole fish, fillets, steaks or cutlets can be simply cooked without any additional liquid other than perhaps a few drops of lemon juice and a little melted butter or sunflower margarine, or coated with the latter if preferred. A sprinkling of seasonings or herbs will enhance the flavour and appearance. Alternatively, fish may be poached in liquid, and a little soured cream, curd cheese or yoghurt stirred in at the end if a well-flavoured sauce is required. Oily fish such as mackerel and herrings can be coated in wholewheat breadcrumbs or rolled oats and dotted with a little butter or margarine, although the coating will not become crisp unless using a browning dish (see Mackerel in Oatmeal page 49).

Test fish and shellfish regularly during cooking as they can easily overcook. Remove the fish when barely done and then allow a standing period to finish cooking. To ensure that the fish cooks evenly, arrange the thicker portions near the edge of the dish with the thinner parts towards the centre. When cooking more than one at a time, the tail ends of thin fillets or whole fish may be overlapped or placed head-to-tail to prevent overcooking of these thinner parts. Alternatively, thin strips of aluminium foil may be wrapped around the head and tail-end of whole fish or the thinner ends of fillets for half the cooking period. For best results, cover the containers and rearrange the fish or turn the dish halfway through the cooking time, although this may not be necessary if you have a microwave cooker with a turntable.

1 medium onion, finely
  chopped
275ml (½pt) dry white wine
1 lemon, juice
4 × 15ml tbsp (4tbsp) chopped
  parsley
4 × 15ml tbsp (4tbsp) olive oil
1 small bay leaf
salt and pepper
12 large scallops, cleaned
2 medium ripe avocados,
  halved and stoned
150ml (¼pt) soured cream
2 × 5ml tsp (2tsp) fresh
  chopped tarragon or ½ ×
  5ml tsp (½tsp) dried
  tarragon
pinch chilli powder

Scallops with avocado dressing *(serves 4)*   *colour opposite*
POWER LEVEL: 100% (FULL)

1   Mix together the onion, wine, half the lemon juice, parsley, oil, bay leaf and salt and pepper in a large dish to make a marinade. Add the scallops, cover and cook for 6–9 min until the scallops are just cooked, taking care not to overcook.
2   Remove the scallops from the marinade using a draining spoon and slice thickly. Place the scallops in a serving dish and pour the marinade over them. Allow to cool, then chill slightly.
3   Prepare the dressing by scooping the flesh out of the avocados and placing it in a food processor or blender with the remaining lemon juice, soured cream, tarragon, chilli powder and salt and pepper to taste. Blend until smooth and transfer to a serving dish and chill in the refrigerator.
4   Serve the scallops with the dressing handed separately.

Fish cooking chart

Fish	Cooking time 100% (full)	Fish	Cooking time 100% (full)
bass 450g (1lb)	5–7 min	kipper 1 medium	1–2 min
bream 900g (2lb)	10–12 min	mackerel 450g (1lb)	5 min
cod fillets 450g (1lb)	4–5 min	plaice fillets 450g (1lb)	4 min
cod steaks 450g (1lb)	6 min	salmon steaks 450g (1lb)	4–5 min
crab claws 450g (1lb)	2–3 min	salmon trout 900g (2lb)	8–10 min
haddock fillets 450g (1lb)	4–5 min	scampi 450g (1lb)	2–3 min
haddock steaks 450g (1lb)	4–5 min	sole 450g (1lb)	4 min
hake steaks 450g (1lb)	7 min	trout 450g (1lb)	7 min

1 bulb fennel, about 225g (8oz), trimmed and sliced
1 medium leek, trimmed and sliced
225g (8oz) tomatoes, skinned and chopped
salt and pepper
1 × 15ml tbsp (1tbsp) fresh chopped majoram or 1 × 5ml tsp (1tsp) dried marjoram
4 cod steaks, 175–225g (6–8oz) each

Cod steaks with fennel *(serves 4)*
POWER LEVEL: 100% (FULL)

1 Place the fennel and leek together in a large bowl or dish. Cover and cook for 5 min, stirring once during cooking.
2 Add the tomatoes, salt and pepper and herbs. Mix well together, cover and cook for a further 4 min, stirring once.
3 Place the cod steaks in a large dish and season lightly. Spoon the vegetables over the fish and cover. Cook for 10–12 min.
4 Allow to stand for a few minutes before serving hot.

450g (1lb) potatoes
pinch salt
150ml (¼pt) water
450g (1lb) kipper fillets
25g (1oz) sunflower margarine
25g (1oz) bran
1 × 15ml tbsp (1tbsp) chopped parsley
salt and pepper
sunflower oil
for garnish: small sprigs parsley

Kipper fish cakes *(serves 4)*
POWER LEVEL: 100% (FULL)

1 Peel the potatoes and cut them into 50–75g (2–3oz) pieces. Place them in a bowl with a pinch of salt and the water. Cover and cook for 12–14 min until tender, stirring once during cooking. Drain and mash.
2 Cook the kippers on a plate covered with pierced clingfilm for 6–8 min. Allow to cool slightly, then skin and flake the fish.
3 Add the margarine and bran to the mashed potato with the parsley and seasoning to taste. Add the flaked kippers and mix well together. Shape the mixture into 8 rounds.
4 Preheat a large browning dish for 6 min. Brush the surface with oil and cook the fish cakes for 4 min. Turn them over and cook for a further 2–3 min. Garnish with parsley sprigs before serving hot.

Moules marinière (serves 2) *colour page 43*
POWER LEVEL: 100% (FULL)

550ml (1pt) mussels
25g (1oz) sunflower margarine
1 small onion, finely chopped
1 small carrot, diced
1 piece celery stick, finely chopped
bouquet garni
salt and pepper
1 wine glass white wine
1–2 × 5ml tsp (1–2tsp) wholewheat flour
for garnish: 2 × 5ml tsp (2tsp) freshly chopped parsley

1 Scrub the mussels and rinse well in cold water. Discard any which are broken or not tightly closed, and scrape away the beards or tufts of hair with a sharp knife.
2 Melt the margarine in a large bowl for 1 min. Add the vegetables, cover and cook for 2 min. Add the bouquet garni, seasoning and white wine, cover and cook for 2 min until boiling. Add the mussels, cover and cook until the shells are open, 3–3½ min approximately, tossing well halfway through.
3 Place the mussels on a serving dish. Strain their liquid into a small bowl and blend in the flour. Cook for 1–2 min until thickened and pour over the mussels.
4 Serve hot garnished with chopped parsley.

DO NOT FREEZE

Chinese red mullet (serves 4)
POWER LEVEL: 100% (FULL)

4 red mullet, weighing about 225–350g (8–12oz) each, cleaned and de-scaled
1 onion, finely sliced
225g (8oz) white or green cabbage, finely shredded
small piece root ginger, peeled and grated
1 clove garlic, crushed
2 × 15ml tbsp (2tbsp) soy sauce
½ lemon, juice
salt and pepper
100g (4oz) beansprouts
for garnish: fresh coriander and lemon butterflies

1 Wash the fish and pat them dry with kitchen paper towel.
2 Place the onion, cabbage, ginger and garlic in a shallow oval dish large enough to take the 4 fish. Cover and cook for 6 min, stirring once during cooking.
3 Add the soy sauce, lemon juice and salt and pepper to taste. Arrange the fish on the bed of vegetables, cover the dish and cook for 3–4 min. Rearrange the fish in the dish, re-cover and cook for a further 3–4 min.
4 Add the beansprouts and cook, uncovered, for a further 1½–2 min. Garnish with fresh coriander and lemon butterflies and serve immediately.

Note: *Small red snappers may also be used in this dish*

175g (6oz) wholewheat lasagne
1 litre (1¾pt) boiling water,
  approximately
1 × 15ml tbsp (1tbsp) oil
1 × 5ml tsp (1tsp) salt
50g (2oz) butter or sunflower
  margarine
1 small onion, finely chopped
1 medium red pepper, deseeded
  and diced
50g (2oz) wholewheat flour
550ml (1pt) milk
450g (1lb) smoked fish fillet,
  cod or haddock
freshly ground black pepper
100g (4oz) peeled prawns
salt, optional
50g (2oz) cheddar cheese,
  grated
paprika for sprinkling

Smoked fish and prawn lasagne *(serves 4–6)* *colour opposite*
POWER LEVEL: 100% (FULL)

1 Place the lasagne leaves in a large oblong dish. Add boiling water, oil and salt. Cover and cook for 8–10 min. Allow to stand for a few minutes. Drain the lasagne and pat dry with kitchen paper towel.
2 Melt the butter or margarine in a large bowl or jug for 1–1½ min, add the onion and red pepper, cover and cook for 4–4½ min until tender. Stir in the flour and gradually add the milk.
3 Cut the fish into bite-size pieces and add to the sauce with the black pepper. Cover and cook for 9–10 min until cooked and thickened, stirring 2–3 times throughout. Add the prawns and cook for a further 2 min. Adjust the seasoning.
4 Layer the sauce and lasagne in the oblong dish, beginning and ending with the sauce. Sprinkle with the cheese.
5 Cook for a further 5 min until heated through and the cheese is melted. Sprinkle with paprika and serve hot.

1 red snapper (or bream),
  weighing about 900g (2lb),
  cleaned and de-scaled
4 bay leaves
salt and pepper
3 oranges
3 lemons
for garnish: few orange and
  lemon slices

Red snapper St Clements *(serves 3–4)* *colour opposite*
POWER LEVEL: 60% AND 100% (FULL)

1 Make 8 small slits in the skin of the fish. Break 2 of the bay leaves into quarters and place a piece of bay leaf into each slit. Rub the fish gently with your fingers to bring out the flavour of the bay. Place the remaining bay leaves into the cavity of the fish.
2 Place the bream in a large dish, cover and cook for 15–18 min on 60% setting. Allow to stand while preparing the fruit sauce.
3 Cut all the rind and pith from the oranges and lemons then cut the fruits into segments. Place the segments with any juice in a small dish, cover and heat for 3–4 min on 100% (full) setting.
4 Garnish the bream with a few orange and lemon slices and serve with the fruit sauce handed separately.

1 × 15ml tbsp (1tbsp) mustard
  seeds
1 small piece ginger, peeled
  and grated
1 green chilli, finely chopped
½ × 5ml tsp (½tsp) turmeric
pinch chilli powder
salt
½ × 5ml tsp (½tsp) light
  muscovado sugar
1 × 15ml tbsp (1tbsp) olive oil
½ × 5ml tsp (½tsp) cumin
  seeds
450g (1lb) king prawns, shelled
for garnish: 1 × 15ml tbsp
  (1tbsp) chopped coriander
  leaves or snipped parsley

Spiced baked prawns *(serves 2–3)*
POWER LEVEL: 100% (FULL)

1 Grind together the mustard seeds, ginger and green chilli in a pestle and mortar, food processor or blender. Add the turmeric, chilli powder, salt and sugar. Mix well together.
2 Heat the oil in a bowl for 2 min, add the cumin seeds and cook for 2 min. Add the spice mixture and blend well together.
3 Add the prawns and coat in the sauce. Cover and cook for 4 min, stirring once throughout. Serve piping hot sprinkled with the chopped coriander leaves or snipped parsley.

Smoked Fish and Prawn Lasagne (above); Red Snapper St Clements (above)

675g (1½lb) fresh cod
salt for sprinkling
1 × 15ml tbsp (1tbsp) seasoned
  wholewheat flour
4 × 15ml tbsp (4tbsp)
  sunflower oil
2 small onions, sliced
2 large green peppers, deseeded
  and sliced
450g (1lb) tomatoes, skinned
  and quartered
salt and freshly ground black
  pepper
1 × 15ml tbsp (1tbsp) freshly
  chopped oregano or parsley

Cod romana *(serves 4–6)*
POWER LEVEL: 100% (FULL)

The fish is lightly pre-fried using a browning dish

1 Remove the skin from the cod, slice the flesh from the bone and cut into 3.75cm (1½in) pieces.
2 Sprinkle the fish with salt and leave for 30 min to draw out some of the moisture. Rinse well in cold water, pat the pieces dry and toss in the seasoned flour.
3 Preheat the browning dish for 6–8 min. Add 2 × 15ml tbsp (2tbsp) oil and heat for 1 min. Add the fish, pressing it down against the hot base of the dish for 10–15 sec with a heatproof spatula. Turn the pieces over, press down well again, cover and cook for 2 min.
4 Drain well and remove the cod pieces. Add the remaining 2 × 15ml tbsp (2tbsp) oil to the dish, stir in the onions, cover and cook for 2 min. Add the peppers, cover and cook for 6 min.
5 Add the cod and tomatoes to the vegetables and mix carefully together. Season to taste, cover and cook for 4 min.
6 Serve hot sprinkled with chopped oregano or parsley.

1 medium aubergine, weighing
  about 225g (8oz)
1 large onion, chopped
2 × 15ml tbsp (2tbsp)
  sunflower oil
1 × 15ml tbsp (1tbsp) tomato
  paste
2 × 5ml tsp (2tsp) fresh
  chopped oregano or ½ × 5ml
  tsp (½tsp) dried oregano
25g (1oz) wholewheat
  breadcrumbs
225g (8oz) peeled prawns
salt and freshly ground black
  pepper
2 × 15ml tbsp (2tbsp) grated
  cheddar cheese
1 × 15ml tbsp (1tbsp) grated
  parmesan cheese
for garnish: few unpeeled
  prawns and sprigs parsley
for serving: freshly cooked
  wholewheat pasta and a green
  salad

Prawns with aubergines *(serves 3–4)*   *colour page 67*
POWER LEVEL: 100% (FULL)

1 Score the aubergine or prick with a fork, and cook, uncovered, for 7–8 min until tender. Leave to cool slightly.
2 Place the onion and oil in a large bowl or dish, cover and cook for 6 min, stirring once throughout. Stir in the tomato paste, oregano, breadcrumbs and prawns. Add seasoning to taste.
3 Cut the cooked aubergine in half, scoop out and coarsely chop the flesh, disgarding the skin.
4 Stir the aubergine into the prawn mixture. Pile into a suitable serving dish and sprinkle with the grated cheeses.
5 Cook, uncovered, for 3–4 min until hot through or brown the top under a hot grill. Garnish with a few unpeeled prawns and sprigs of parsley before serving with wholewheat pasta and a green salad.

Stuffed herrings with gooseberry sauce (*serves 4*)
POWER LEVEL: 100% (FULL)

1 Clean and bone the herrings or ask the fishmonger to do it for you.
2 Melt the margarine in a bowl for 1 min. Add the onion, toss well in the margarine, cover and cook for 3–4 min until tender.
3 Stir in the breadcrumbs, seasonings and herbs. Add sufficient hot water to bind the stuffing together.
4 Divide the stuffing between the herrings, re-shape the fish and place head-to-tail in a large shallow casserole dish, overlapping slightly to protect the tail ends, or alternatively cover these thinner parts with small, smooth pieces of aluminium foil. Cover with greaseproof paper.
5 Cook for 8–10 min, rearranging the fish halfway through if necessary, by placing the centre ones to the outside. Leave to stand, covered, for 5 min.
6 Place the gooseberry sauce in a serving bowl or jug and heat through if necessary for 2–3 min, although the sauce may also be served cold.
7 Garnish the herrings with lemon slices and serve with the sauce handed separately.

4 herrings
25g (1oz) sunflower margarine
1 small onion, finely chopped
100g (4oz) wholewheat breadcrumbs
salt and freshly ground black pepper
1 × 15ml tbsp (1tbsp) chopped parsley
2 × 5ml tsp (2tsp) chopped fresh mixed herbs or ½ × 5ml tsp (½tsp) dried mixed herbs
2–3 × 15ml tbsp (2–3tbsp) hot water
275ml (½pt) gooseberry sauce (fruit sauce, page 25)
for garnish: lemon slices

Bass with spring vegetables (*serves 4–6*)   *colour page 119*
POWER LEVEL: 100% (FULL)

1 Scrub and score the potato. Place on a piece of kitchen paper and cook for 4 min or until soft. Allow to cool slightly, then peel and dice.
2 Place the leek, carrot, celery and beans in a covered dish with 2 × 15ml tbsp (2tbsp) salted water. Cook for 5–6 min, stirring once. The vegetables should be cooked but remain crisp.
3 Arrange the bass in a single layer in a dish, add the soured cream and season lightly. Cover and cook for 7–10 min. Using a draining spoon or slice, remove the fish.
4 Drain any liquid from the vegetables and reserve. Arrange the fish and the vegetables in a serving dish.
5 Purée the cream, the vegetable liquid and the potato in a blender or food processor. Add milk if the sauce is too thick. Season and add the chives.
6 Pour the sauce over the fish and vegetables and reheat for 2–3 min.

1 potato, weighing about 175g (6oz)
1 small leek, trimmed and sliced
1 medium carrot, cut into fine matchsticks
1 large stick celery, trimmed and cut into fine matchsticks
4 green beans, trimmed and cut into 2.5cm (1in) slices
675g (1½lb) bass, skinned and cut into 4 pieces
150ml (¼pt) soured cream
salt and pepper
milk
1 × 15ml tbsp (1tbsp) chopped chives

Mackerel in oatmeal (*serves 4*)
POWER LEVEL: 100% (FULL)

The mackerel are cooked in a browning dish

1 Clean the fish and remove heads and tails. Wash in cold water and dry.
2 Brush the fish with the 15g (½oz) melted margarine, then dip in the oatmeal or rolled oats, pressing the oats well onto the fish.
3 Preheat the browning dish for 6–8 min, depending on its size, and add half the melted margarine. Heat for a further 1 min and then add 2 of the fish. Cook, uncovered, for 2 min, turn the fish over, cover and cook for a further 2–3 min. Remove from the dish and keep warm.
4 Remove any dripping from the browning dish, preheat for 3–4 min, and cook the remaining 2 fish as described above.
5 Serve hot sprinkled with plenty of chopped parsley and garnished with lemon wedges.

4 mackerel, weighing about 225–275g (8–10oz) each
15g (½oz) sunflower margarine, melted
salt and pepper
fine oatmeal or rolled oats
25–50g (1–2oz) sunflower margarine, melted
for garnish: chopped parsley and lemon wedges

450g (1lb) smoked haddock
    fillets, skinned
450g (1lb) fresh haddock fillets,
    skinned (try to choose small,
    evenly sized thin fillets or
    trim to shape)
1 small onion, finely chopped
100g (4oz) curd cheese
1 × 15ml tbsp (1tbsp) chopped
    parsley
salt and pepper
1 × 5ml tsp (1tsp) curry powder
1 × 5ml tsp (1tsp) turmeric
for garnish: sprigs watercress
for serving: thin slices of
    wholewheat bread

Haddock turban (*serves 8*)   *colour opposite*
POWER LEVEL: 100% (FULL) AND 60%

Serve this dish as a starter to a meal

1   Lightly oil a 17.5cm (7in) microwave ring mould. Line the base and sides
    with alternate fillets of smoked and white fish, overlapping the fillets and
    using about three-quarters of the fish.
2   Place the remaining fish in a covered dish with the onion and cook on
    100% (full) setting for 3–5 min. Cool slightly and flake the fish.
3   Beat in the curd cheese, parsley and seasoning. Add the curry powder
    and turmeric and mix well together.
4   Spoon the mixture carefully into the prepared ring mould. Smooth the
    surface with the back of a spoon, then fold the fish fillets over the filling.
5   Cover the dish and cook on 60% setting for 9–12 min. Allow the turban to
    cool. Drain off any surplus liquid and turn the turban out onto a serving
    plate.
6   Chill well and garnish with sprigs of watercress before serving with thin
    slices of wholewheat bread.

2 grapefruit
1 × 15ml tbsp (1tbsp) olive oil
100g (4oz) cashew nuts
4 trout, about 350g (12oz) each,
    cleaned and trimmed
salt and pepper
for garnish: watercress

Trout with grapefruit and cashews (*serves 4*)   *colour page 39*
POWER LEVEL: 100% (FULL)

1   Remove all peel and pith from the grapefruits and cut the flesh into
    segments. Reserve any juice from the fruit.
2   Heat the oil on a large oval heatproof plate for 2 min. Add the cashews,
    toss over in the oil and cook for 3–4 min, uncovered, or until browned,
    stirring once throughout.
3   Stuff each trout with some of the grapefruit segments. Arrange the fish
    head-to-tail on a plate or in a large shallow dish and sprinkle with the nuts.
    Season lightly with salt and pepper and pour over any juice from the
    grapefruits.
4   Cover the plate with kitchen paper towel and cook the trout for 10–14
    min, rearranging the fish on the plate halfway through cooking if
    necessary. Garnish with watercress before serving hot.

675g (1½lb) monkfish, skinned
1½ lemons
4 eggs
150g (5oz) can tomato paste
salt and pepper
for garnish: parsley and tomato
    and lemon slices
for serving: mayonnaise
    (page 22)

Fish pâté (*serves 6–8*)   *colour opposite*
POWER LEVEL: 100% (FULL) AND 30%

*This pâté has a texture and taste resembling that of lobster, a clever illusion as
monkfish is cheaper than lobster*

1   Place the fish fillets in a dish with the juice of 1 lemon. Chop the flesh of
    the ½ lemon and scatter it over the fish. Cover the dish and cook for
    6–7 min, rearranging the fillets halfway through cooking if necessary.
    Allow to stand for 5 min before draining off the liquid.
2   Beat the eggs together with the tomato paste and seasoning. Chop the
    fish into small pieces. Mix with the tomato and egg mixture and pour into
    a shallow microwave loaf dish.
3   Cover the dish and cook on 30% setting for 15–20 min until set. Allow to
    cool and then chill in the refrigerator.
4   Turn out onto a serving plate and garnish with sprigs of parsley and
    tomato and lemon slices. Serve with mayonnaise.

Haddock Turban (above);
Fish Pâté (above)

Meat, Poultry and Game

Meat is one of the best sources of protein available and there is little reason why a wholefood cook need exclude it from the diet if there is access to naturally reared meat from a known local butcher or farm. However, it may be that as other forms of protein are introduced more into the diet, meat plays a less important role. Good quality prime cuts are ideal for the wholefood microwave cook as the fast cooking methods ensure retention of the natural flavours. Another advantage of microwave cooking is that virtually no additional fat is needed for meat and poultry to remain moist and succulent. Game is one of the most natural foods in this category and some types such as rabbit and pigeon are inexpensive and now widely available.

Cooking

For best results, a joint should be regular in shape so that it will have a better appearance and cook more evenly—rolled joints or top leg of lamb or pork are ideal. If the meat is not uniform in size, the narrower sections may be covered with a smooth piece of aluminium foil for half the cooking time. Poultry and game birds should have the wings and legs tied closely to the body, and any projecting parts should be protected by covering them with foil.

Seasonings should be limited to spices and herbs, as salt attracts moisture and can have a toughening effect on the outside of the meat during cooking. If in any doubt, leave the seasonings to the end of the cooking time. Meat can be open roasted by placing it on an upturned small, flat dish or plate which serves as a trivet inside the roasting dish. Special microwave roasting dishes are now available. These serve a similar purpose as the trivet in keeping the meat out of the juices during cooking. The open roasting method allows moisture to escape and gives a crisper finish to the outside of the meat. Cover the dish with greaseproof paper or kitchen paper towel to help prevent splashings of fat onto the oven interior. Alternatively, roasting bags may be used to cook joints, but remember that wire ties must not be used—use string or rubber bands instead. The roasting bag should be pierced or slit at the base so that the juices will run out into the cooking container away from the meat.

Larger joints should be turned over at least once during the cooking period, and a joint which has fat on one side only should be placed fat side down at the beginning of cooking and turned over halfway through so that the fat is then on the top. If cooking joints on 100% (full) setting, a standing time of 10–25 min halfway through cooking will help to give a more even result—particularly important for joints over 2kg (4lb) in weight. If using a 70% setting on a variable power control model, this standing period halfway through is not necessary. Most joints should be allowed to stand for 5–20 min at the end of the cooking period, left in the roasting bag or covered in aluminium foil to retain the heat. However, if the joint is cooked to the desired degree on completion of the cooking time, it is not necessary to let it stand.

If the total cooking time is 15 min or more the joint will brown naturally, but for extra browning the joint may be placed in a conventional oven at a high temperature for 10–15 min at the end of the microwave cooking period, or placed under a hot grill. The careful use of sauces, paprika or seasonings painted or sprinkled onto the surface of the meat will give a more attractive colour if preferred. Steaks, chops and escalopes may be browned during

cooking by using a browning dish, or alternatively finished off under a hot grill after cooking by microwave.

The cooking times given in the following charts are when using a 100% (full) setting and a 70% setting. For those microwave cookers with a 'roast' setting, it is advisable to check with the manufacturer's recommendations regarding cooking times. If you have a microwave with 'full' and 'defrost' settings only, the joint may be cooked for half the time on 100% (full) setting and then reduced to the 'defrost' setting for the remaining time. Alternatively, some joints benefit from a slow cooking process using the 'defrost' setting throughout, in which case the cooking time will be double to treble that for 100% (full) setting. Much depends on the time available and your own preferences.

The use of a meat thermometer is helpful to determine the temperature at the centre of the food, particularly when cooking larger cuts and joints. Only specially designed thermometers for microwave cookers may be left inside the oven while it is operating. Ordinary meat thermometers must not be used in the microwave, but can be inserted into the centre of the joint when the latter has been taken out of the oven cavity. The following temperatures after the final standing time will help you to assess whether the meat is cooked. If your microwave cooker has the facility of a probe, set it to the temperatures given below although it is advisable to check with the manufacturer's instructions before using.

beef	
rare	60°C (140°F)
medium	70°C (160°F)
well done	80°C (175°F)
lamb	80°C (175°F)
pork	80°C (175°F)
veal	80°C (175°F)
poultry and game birds	80–85°C (175–185°F)

When braising, casseroling or stewing meat, poultry or game, best results are obtained using a lower 50% or 30% setting for the total cooking time. This will give the longer cooking period required for tenderising the meat and will also allow sufficient time for the food flavourings and seasonings to blend. The container should be covered with a lid for the entire cooking process to retain moisture and to prevent the liquid in the casserole from evaporating. As the casserole is being cooked by microwave energy from all directions inside the oven—the top as well as the sides and base—it is best to ensure that the food is well covered with the cooking liquid so that the meat at the top does not overcook and toughen.

Points to remember

★ A joint will have a better appearance and cook more evenly if it is a regular shape.
★ Smooth pieces of aluminium foil may be used to protect the thinner or narrower ends of meat during cooking.
★ Meat can benefit from a standing time at the end of the cooking process, but larger joints also require a standing time halfway through their cooking period. This is not necessary though, if using a lower power level for cooking, ie 70% setting.
★ In addition, larger joints should be turned over halfway through the cooking cycle.
★ The tenderness of meat casseroles is often improved if the dish is left to cool after microwave cooking and then reheated when required.
★ The times given on the following charts are for both lower and higher output microwave cookers; models with lower output will require the longer times, those with a higher output will require the shorter times, ie beef, medium, 5–7 min per ½kg (1lb).
★ Allow an extra 1 min per ½kg (1lb) when cooking stuffed joints, or poultry or game birds.

Meat, poultry and game cooking chart

Meat, Poultry, Game	Cooking time per ½kg (1lb) 100% (full)	Cooking time per ½kg (1lb) 70% setting
beef rolled, boned 1½–2kg (3–4lb)	rare = 4–6 min med = 5–7 min well = 6–8 min stand for 15–25 min	10–11 min 11–13 min 12–14 min stand for 10–15 min
beef joints on bone 2–3kg (4–6lb)	rare = 4–6 min med = 5–7 min well = 6–8 min stand for 15–25 min	10–11 min 11–13 min 12–14 min stand for 20 min
capon, whole 3–4kg (6–8lb)	7–9 min stand for 25–35 min	10–12 min stand for 10–15 min
chicken, whole 1–2½kg (2–5lb)	5–7 min stand for 15–25 min	9–10 min stand for 5 min
chicken joints ¾–1kg (1½–2lb)	6–8 min stand for 5 min	8–10 min stand for 5 min

Natural Yoghurt (page 36) with Fruit Sauce (page 25); Turkey Strogonoff (page 57); Tomato Soup (page 22)

Meat, Poultry, Game	Cooking time per ½kg (1lb) 100% (full)	Cooking time per ½kg (1lb) 70% setting
duckling, whole 2–2½kg (4–5lb)	5–7 min stand for 15–25 min	9–11 min stand for 5 min
goose, whole 2½–3kg (5–6lb)	6–8 min stand for 15–25 min	10–12 min stand for 5–10 min
hare, saddle ¾–1kg (1½–2lb)	—	8–10 min stand for 15 min
lamb 1¼–1¾kg (2½–3½lb)	7–9 min stand for 15–30 min	11–13 min stand for 20 min
partridge, whole 350g (12oz)	—	11–12 min stand for 15 min
pheasant, whole ¾–1½kg (1¾–3lb)	—	11–12 min stand for 15 min
pork or ham 1½–3kg (3–6lb)	7–9 min stand for 15–30 min	12–14 min stand for 20 min
turkey, whole 3–4kg (6–8lb)	7–9 min stand for 25–35 min	10–12 min stand for 10–15 min
turkey, jointed 1–1¼kg (2–2½lb)	7–9 min stand for 10 min	9–10 min stand for 5 min
turkey, joint 1–2kg (2–4lb)	8–10 min stand for 15 min	11–13 min stand for 10–15 min
veal 1½–2½kg (3–5lb)	7–9 min stand for 15–30 min	11–13 min stand for 20 min
venison, joint 1½–2½kg (3–5lb)	—	11–13 min stand for 15–20 min

Browning dish chart
POWER LEVEL: 100% (FULL)

After preheating the browning dish as indicated in the chart below, up to 1 × 15ml tbsp (1tbsp) sunflower oil may be brushed over the hot surface of the dish before adding the food. Using a heatproof spatula, press the meat down against the hot base of the dish to ensure maximum contact and browning of the underside of the food.

Food	Preheat	First side	Second side
4 bacon rashers	5–6 min	1 min	30–45 sec
2 chicken pieces each 225g (8oz)	5–6 min	5 min	3–5 min

Food	Preheat	First side	Second side
1 gammon steak 175g (6oz)	5–6 min	3 min	3–4 min
6 hamburgers or rissoles each 75–100g (3–4oz)	6–7 min	2 min	6–8 min
4 lamb chops each 100g (4oz)	5–6 min	3 min	8–10 min
2 pork chops each 225g (8oz)	5–6 min	3 min	8–10 min
1 steak 175–200g (6–7oz)	6–7 min	1½–2 min	1½–2 min

Turkey stroganoff (serves 6–8)   colour page 55
POWER LEVEL: 100% (FULL) AND 60%

40g (1½oz) butter or sunflower margarine
1 onion, thinly sliced
175g (6oz) mushrooms, sliced
675g (1½lb) turkey breast fillet, cut into strips
3 × 15ml tbsp (3tbsp) wholewheat flour
salt and freshly ground black pepper
150ml (¼pt) soured cream
for garnish: chopped parsley or paprika

1   Melt the butter or margarine in a large dish for 1–2 min. Add the onion, cover and cook for 2 min. Stir in the mushrooms and continue to cook for a further 2–3 min.
2   Toss the strips of turkey in the flour and add them to the vegetables. Stir well and cook, uncovered, for 9–12 min on 100% (full). Stir once or twice during cooking.
3   Add salt and freshly ground black pepper to taste and stir in the soured cream. Heat the dish for a further 3–4 min on 60% setting, stirring halfway through.
4   Serve hot garnished with a little chopped parsley or a sprinkling of paprika.

Double loin chops with prunes and walnuts (serves 2)
POWER LEVEL: 100% (FULL) AND 60%

75g (3oz) prunes
water
2 double loin chops, approximately 175–200g (6–7oz) each
1 large onion, chopped
½ red pepper, deseeded and diced
salt and pepper
275ml (½pt) apple juice
25g (1oz) wholewheat flour
50g (2oz) walnuts, roughly chopped
1 × 15ml tbsp (1tbsp) dark demerara sugar

The chops are browned in a browning dish

1   Cover the prunes with water in a small bowl or dish. Heat, covered, for 5 min on 100% (full) and allow to stand for 10 min.
2   Preheat a large browning dish for 6 min. Add the chops, cook for 2 min, turn them over and cook for a further 2 min. Leave them on the browning dish to keep warm.
3   Cook the onion and pepper in a large covered casserole dish for 4 min, stirring once during cooking. Drain the prunes, remove the stones and add the prunes to the dish with a little seasoning.
4   Place the chops on top of the vegetable and prunes and add the apple juice. Cover and cook for 10 min on 60% setting. Remove the chops to a warm serving plate.
5   Blend the flour with a little of the cooking liquid and stir it into the sauce. Cook for 2–3 min on 100% (full) until boiling and thickened, stirring every minute. Adjust the seasoning.
6   Add the chopped nuts and sugar to the sauce. Serve with some of the sauce poured over the chops and the remainder handed separately.

1 chicken, weighing about
   1½kg (3lb)
225g (8oz) clear honey
1 × 15ml tbsp (1tbsp) chopped
   fresh tarragon or 1 × 5ml tsp
   (1tsp) dried tarragon
2 bay leaves
2 lemons, grated rind and juice
3.75cm (1½in) piece fresh
   ginger, grated
salt and pepper
½ × 5ml tsp (½tsp) paprika
for garnish: sprigs tarragon

Honey and tarragon roast chicken *(serves 6–8)*   *colour opposite*
POWER LEVEL: 100% (FULL) AND 70%

1 Remove any excess fat from the chicken and tie the legs close to the body with string, wooden skewers or cocktail sticks. Protect the drumsticks with small smooth pieces of aluminium foil.
2 Place the remaining ingredients except the garnish in a casserole dish. Heat for 2–3 min, then stir well until blended.
3 Place the chicken in the casserole dish and baste with the sauce. Cover and cook for 28–35 min on 70% setting or until the inside thigh temperature registers 80–85°C (175–185°F) when using a meat thermometer. Baste the chicken occasionally during the cooking time.
4 Allow to stand for 5 min before serving garnished with the sprigs of tarragon. If preferred, the chicken may be jointed before placing on a serving plate or dish and coating with the sauce.

1 onion, chopped
1 clove garlic, crushed
450g (1lb) lamb's liver
salt and freshly ground black
   pepper
2 × 15ml tbsp (2tbsp)
   wholewheat flour
275ml (½pt) boiling stock
2 × 15ml tbsp (2tbsp) tomato
   paste
2 rashers bacon, de-rinded and
   diced
100g (4oz) wholewheat
   breadcrumbs
1 small onion, very finely
   chopped or minced
40g (1½oz) nuts, chopped,
   (walnuts, brazils, hazel nuts)

Crispy topped liver casserole *(serves 4)*   *colour opposite*
POWER LEVEL: 100% (FULL)

After cooking in the microwave the casserole is browned under a hot grill

1 Cook the onion and garlic in a covered casserole dish for 3 min, stirring once throughout.
2 Wipe the liver with paper towel if necessary. Add seasoning to the flour and toss the liver slices in it. Add the liver to the casserole dish.
3 Blend the stock with the tomato paste and pour over the liver. Cover and cook for 10–12 min, stirring the dish or rearranging the liver halfway through. Allow to stand for 3–4 min.
4 Place the bacon on a plate or in a dish and cook for 2–3 min. Mix in the breadcrumbs, finely chopped or minced onion and the nuts. Add seasoning to taste.
5 Sprinkle the mixture over the top of the liver casserole and brown under a preheated grill.

4 large or 8 small slices of
   topside or silverside of beef
1–2 × 15ml tbsp (1–2tbsp)
   mild or grained mustard
1 onion, finely chopped
1 red pepper, deseeded and
   thinly sliced
2 × 15ml tbsp (2tbsp) chopped
   parsley
2 × 15ml tbsp (2tbsp)
   sunflower oil
salt, pepper and paprika
275–425ml (½–¾pt) boiling
   vegetable stock
2 × 15ml tbsp (1tbsp) tomato
   paste
for garnish: chopped parsley
for serving: creamed or jacket
   potatoes or noodles and a
   salad

Beef paupiettes *(serves 4)*   *colour opposite*
POWER LEVEL: 100% (FULL) AND 30%

1 Flatten the slices of beef by beating firmly with the heel of your hand. Spread each slice with mustard and sprinkle with a little chopped onion.
2 Arrange the red pepper on the beef and sprinkle with the parsley. Roll up each slice and secure with a wooden cocktail stick or string.
3 Place the oil in a dish just large enough to take the paupiettes. Arrange them in the dish and brush with the oil. Cover and cook for 4 min. Sprinkle with salt, pepper and a good shake of paprika.
4 Mix the stock with the tomato paste and pour over the paupiettes. Cover and cook on 30% setting for 1–1¼ hr, turning the meat over in the dish once or twice during cooking.
5 Remove the meat from the dish and keep warm. Heat the juices on 100% (full) for 10–15 min to reduce to a rich gravy. Replace the paupiettes in the dish, spoon over the gravy and garnish with chopped parsley before serving with creamed or jacket potatoes, or noodles and a salad.

Honey and Tarragon Roast Chicken (above); Beef Paupiettes (above); Crispy Topped Liver Casserole (above)

2 pork chops, about 175g (6oz)
  each
1 onion, grated
1 cooking apple, grated
salt and pepper
1 bay leaf
1 blade mace
1 × 15ml tbsp (1tbsp) dark
  demerara sugar

Pork chops with apple and mace *(serves 2)*
POWER LEVEL: 100% (FULL) AND 70%

1 Preheat a browning dish on 100% (full) for 8 min. Press the chops onto the hot surface of the dish with a heatproof spatula, turn the chops over and cook in the microwave for 2 min. Leave on the browning dish to keep warm.
2 Place the grated onion and apple in a large dish with salt and pepper to taste, the herbs and sugar. Cover and cook for 3 min.
3 Add the chops to the dish and toss in the apple mixture. Cover with a lid or pierced clingfilm and cook for 6 min on 70% setting. Allow to stand for 3–4 min before serving hot.

450g (1lb) lamb off the bone—
  neck fillet or cut from the
  leg or shoulder
900g (2lb) onions, finely
  chopped
2 × 15ml tbsp (2tbsp) ground
  coriander
1 × 5ml tsp (1tsp) chilli powder
3 × 15ml tbsp (3tbsp)
  sunflower oil
2 onions, chopped
2 cloves garlic, crushed
2 bay leaves
½ × 5ml tsp (½tsp) turmeric
2 × 15ml tbsp (2tbsp) lemon
  juice
4–5 × 5ml tsp (4–5tsp) garam
  masala
salt
1 × 15ml tbsp (1tbsp) chopped
  coriander leaves or parsley

Do-piaza (spiced lamb with onions) *(serves 4)*   *colour page 87*
POWER LEVEL: 100% (FULL) AND 30%

This delicious indian dish is cooked on a low power setting to allow the flavours to blend. It is best prepared and cooked the day before required

1 Cut the lamb into small cubes or pieces. Layer half the onions into a medium-size casserole and arrange the prepared meat over the top with the ground coriander and chilli powder. Cover with the remaining onions.
2 Cover the dish and cook for 10 min on 100% (full) and a further 50–60 min on 30% setting. Leave to stand until quite cold.
3 Heat the oil in a small bowl for 2 min, add the onion, garlic and bay leaves. Cover and cook for 3–4 min, stirring once throughout. Add the turmeric and cook for a further 1 min.
4 Add the hot onions to the meat and stir well. Reheat the casserole for 6–7 min on 100% (full) setting, stirring occasionally. Add the lemon juice and garam masala and continue to cook for a further 2 min. Stir in salt to taste and serve sprinkled with the chopped coriander or parsley.

175g (6oz) dried chestnuts
boiling water
275ml (½pt) boiling vegetable
  stock
1 small onion
225g (8oz) cooked pheasant
  meat
150ml (¼pt) soured cream
2 × 15ml tbsp (2tbsp)
  mayonnaise (page 22)
½ × 5ml tsp (½tsp) grated
  nutmeg
salt and freshly ground black
  pepper
150ml (¼pt) water, wine or
  stock
1 envelope gelatin
for garnish: watercress
for serving: thinly sliced
  wholewheat toast

Pheasant and chestnut mousse *(serves 8)*
POWER LEVEL: 100% (FULL) AND 50%

Serve as a starter

1 Cover the chestnuts with boiling water in a bowl, cover and cook for 5 min. Allow to stand for 1 hr.
2 Drain the chestnuts, add the boiling stock to them, cover and cook for 10 min on 100% (full) then a further 10–15 min on 50% setting. Purée the chestnuts with the stock in a blender or food processor and reserve.
3 Finely chop the onion and pheasant meat in a blender or food processor or put through a mincer. Add the chestnuts, cream, mayonnaise, nutmeg and seasoning and mix well together.
4 Heat the water, wine or stock for 2 min, add the gelatin and stir well. Heat for a further 15–30 sec until fully dissolved, if necessary. Stir the gelatin into the pheasant mixture.
5 Rinse a 17.5cm (7in) ring mould under cold water, fill with the mousse and smooth the surface. Chill until firm.
6 Turn out onto a serving dish or plate and garnish with watercress. Serve with thinly sliced wholewheat toast.

Pot-braised pork in milk (*serves 6*)
POWER LEVEL: 100% (FULL) AND 70%

900g (2lb) boned leg of pork
1 × 15ml tbsp (1tbsp) coriander
  seeds
2 cloves garlic, cut into slivers
1 × 15ml tbsp (1tbsp) freshly
  chopped tarragon
1.1 litre (2pt) milk,
  approximately
100g (4oz) bacon, de-rinded
  and diced
1 onion, chopped
1 blade mace
50g (2oz) sunflower margarine
50g (2oz) wholewheat flour
salt and pepper
for garnish: chopped parsley

1 Cut any fat from the pork and discard. Place the coriander, garlic and tarragon in the meat, roll up and tie securely with string.
2 Place the pork in a small casserole dish, cover with milk and leave to marinate for 1 hr.
3 Place the bacon, onion and mace in a separate casserole dish and cook, covered, for 4 min, stirring once throughout. Lift the pork from the milk and arrange it on the bed of bacon and onion. Pour over enough milk from the marinade to half fill the dish.
4 Cover and cook for 25–30 min on 70% setting or until the pork is cooked. Turn the pork over in the milk halfway through cooking.
5 Remove the joint to a carving board or plate and allow to stand for 5 min before slicing.
6 Strain the milk from the dish, reserving the bacon and onion. Make the milk up to 550ml (1pt) with extra milk from the marinade (any remaining milk can be used for soups).
7 Melt the margarine in a bowl on 100% (full) for 1½–2 min. Stir in the flour and gradually add the milk. Cook for 5–6 min until boiling and thickened, stirring every minute. Season well to taste with salt and pepper.
8 Arrange the pork slices on a serving plate or dish and sprinkle with the reserved bacon and onion. Coat with some of the sauce and garnish with chopped parsley. Hand any remaining sauce separately.

Rabbit casserole with herb dumplings (*serves 6*)
POWER LEVEL: 100% (FULL) AND 50%

2 onions, chopped
2 cloves garlic, crushed
100g (4oz) bacon, de-rinded
  and diced
1 green pepper, deseeded and
  sliced
675g (1½lb) rabbit, off the
  bone, cut into small pieces
40g (1½oz) wholewheat flour
2 × 5ml tsp (2tsp) mustard
  powder
425ml (¾pt) boiling vegetable
  stock
salt and pepper
2 bay leaves
150ml (¼pt) natural yoghurt

for the dumplings:
175g (6oz) wholewheat flour
2 × 5ml tsp (2tsp) baking
  powder
pinch salt
75g (3oz) suet, grated
1 × 15ml tbsp (1tbsp) fresh
  chopped rosemary
cold water to mix

1 Cook the onion and garlic in a large covered casserole dish for 3 min. Add the bacon and cook for a further 2 min. Add the pepper and rabbit and continue to cook for 6–8 min, stirring once.
2 Stir in the flour and mustard, then gradually add the boiling stock. Add the salt and pepper and bay leaves and cook for 3–4 min until boiling, stirring every minute.
3 Stir the natural yoghurt into the casserole. Cover and cook for 10 min on 100% (full) and a further 25–35 min on 50% setting.
4 For the dumplings, place the flour, baking powder and salt in a bowl. Stir in the suet and rosemary, and mix to a soft manageable dough with cold water. Shape into 12 small dumplings or 6 larger ones, using a little extra flour to prevent sticking if necessary.
5 Correct the seasoning of the rabbit casserole and add the dumplings, arranging them on the top of the dish in a circle if possible. Cover and cook for 7–10 min on 100% (full) until risen and cooked through. Serve immediately.

25g (1oz) sunflower margarine
450g (1lb) jerusalem
  artichokes, sliced
1 × 15ml tbsp (1tbsp) lemon
  juice
oil
675g (1½lb) turkey breast
  fillet, cut into 6 slices
1 leek, trimmed and sliced
1 red pepper, deseeded and cut
  into strips
100g (4oz) cauliflower, cut into
  small florets
salt and pepper
150ml (¼pt) soured cream or
  yoghurt
1 × 15ml tbsp (1tbsp) chopped
  parsley
for serving: tomato sauce
  (page 25)

Turkey with creamed artichokes *(serves 6)* *colour opposite*
POWER LEVEL: 100% (FULL)

The turkey is pre-cooked in a browning dish

1 Melt the margarine in a bowl for 1 min, add the artichokes and lemon juice and toss well. Cover and cook for 9–10 min until tender, stirring once during cooking. Allow to cool slightly.
2 Preheat a large browning dish for 6 min. Brush with oil and add the turkey slices. Cook for 2 min, turn the slices over and cook for a further 2 min. Leave the turkey on the dish to keep warm.
3 Place the leek, pepper and cauliflower in a large dish, cover and cook for 4 min, stirring once throughout. Add the turkey, season to taste, and cook, covered, for a further 9–12 min.
4 Meanwhile, purée the artichokes with the cooking liquid in a blender or food processor with the soured cream or yoghurt. Stir in the parsley and season to taste.
5 Pipe the creamed artichokes into six large rosettes on a large serving platter. Arrange the turkey and vegetables on the dish and reheat for 3–4 min.
6 Serve hot with tomato sauce.

1 goose, 2½–3kg (5–6lb)
  approximately
1 onion, finely sliced
1 large red pepper, sliced
1 wine glass red wine
2 × 5ml tsp (2tsp) paprika
275ml (½pt) boiling vegetable
  stock
bouquet garni
salt and pepper
8 tomatoes, skinned and
  quartered
25g (1oz) wholewheat flour
paprika for sprinkling
for garnish: stuffed olives and
  fried or toasted croûtes

Braised goose with peppers *(serves 4)* *colour opposite*
POWER LEVEL: 70%

1 Wipe the goose and prick the skin well with a fork to allow the fat to drain away during the cooking process.
2 Place the goose breast-side down in a large dish. Protect the wing tips and legs with small, smooth pieces of aluminium foil. Cover with grease-proof paper.
3 Allow 10 min cooking time per ½kg (1lb) weight. Cook for half the calculated time, turning the dish if necessary every 10 min. Pour off and reserve the fat and juices and remove all the pieces of foil.
4 Turn the goose over and continue to cook for the remaining time. Remove the goose from the dish and allow to stand for a few minutes, keeping it warm.
5 Place 2 × 15ml tbsp (2tbsp) of the goose fat into a bowl or dish and add the onion and red pepper. Cover and cook for 10min. Add the wine, paprika, stock, bouquet garni, seasoning, tomatoes and the juices (without fat) from the goose.
6 Test the goose with a skewer—the juices should run clear and the flesh near the bone should be cooked. Carve into portions and replace in the casserole dish with the vegetable mixture, ensuring that the meat is covered with the liquid.
7 Cover and continue to cook for 30 min, turning the dish or rearranging the goose portions as required.
8 Allow to stand for 20 min. Mix 1 × 15ml tbsp (1tbsp) of the stock with the flour and stir into the casserole. Cook for 2–3 min until thickened, stirring once halfway through.
9 Sprinkle with a little paprika. Garnish with the olives and fried or toasted croûtes before serving.

Braised Goose with Peppers (above);
Turkey with Creamed Artichokes
(above)

Note: *Duck may also be cooked and served as above*

1 boned leg or shoulder of lamb,
  weighing about 1½kg (3lb)
  or 1 boneless lamb shoulder
  roast weighing about 1.1kg
  (2½lb)
100g (4oz) cooked long-grain
  brown rice (page 77)
4 lamb's kidneys, skinned,
  cored and chopped
1 small onion, finely chopped
salt and plenty of ground black
  pepper
1 × 15ml tbsp (1tbsp) natural
  yoghurt
paprika
for garnish: sprigs rosemary or
  parsley

Roast lamb stuffed with kidneys and rice *(serves 6)*
POWER LEVEL: 70%

1 Lay the lamb out on a chopping board or work surface, untying it if
   necessary. Mix together the rice, kidneys, onion, salt and pepper and
   yoghurt. Use to stuff the lamb.
2 Roll the meat into a neat parcel and tie into shape with string. Place on a
   roasting rack and sprinkle with black pepper and paprika.
3 Cook at 70% setting for about 45 min (refer to the cooking recommendations in the chart on page 56), or until the internal temperature registers
   80°C (175°F) using a meat thermometer.
4 Allow the meat to stand for 5 min, or cover and keep warm while other
   dishes or vegetables are being cooked. Serve carved into slices and
   garnished with a few sprigs of rosemary or parsley.

900g (2lb) topside or silverside
  of beef, trimmed
6 tomatoes, skinned and puréed
1 leek, finely sliced
1 clove garlic, crushed
2 × 15ml tbsp (2tbsp) tamari
  sauce
1 × 15ml tbsp (1tbsp) dark
  demerara sugar
salt and freshly ground black
  pepper
½ × 5ml tsp (½tsp) chilli
  powder
1 × 15ml tbsp (1tbsp) wine
  vinegar
1 mango, peeled and stoned
for garnish: a little chopped leek
  or spring onion

Beef with mango *(serves 6)*   *colour page 15*
POWER LEVEL: 60%

1 Cut the beef into 12mm (½in) slices, then slice into thin strips. Mix
   together all the remaining ingredients except the mango and pour over the
   beef. Toss well and leave for 1 hr.
2 Place the beef and the marinade in a large flat dish and cook for 15–20
   min on 60% setting, or until the beef is cooked to your liking. Allow to
   stand for 5 min.
3 Slice the mango and stir into the beef. Cover and heat through for
   3–4 min before serving, stirring once. Sprinkle with a little chopped leek
   or spring onion.

1 onion, chopped
275ml (½pt) boiling vegetable
  stock
1–2 × 15ml tbsp (1–2tbsp)
  tamari sauce
pinch nutmeg
1 × 15ml tbsp (1tbsp) fresh
  wholewheat breadcrumbs
salt and pepper
350g (12oz) cooked meat,
  minced
450–675g (1–1½lb) cooked
  potato
25g (1oz) butter or sunflower
  margarine
1 egg, beaten
for garnish: ground nutmeg or
  paprika

Shepherd's pie *(serves 4)*
POWER LEVEL: 100% (FULL)

1 Place the onion in a medium-size dish with the stock and cook for 4 min.
2 Add the sauce, nutmeg, breadcrumbs, seasoning and meat, mixing
   thoroughly.
3 Mash the potato; if the potato is cold, this will be easier if heated for
   2–3 min in the microwave. Add the butter or sunflower margarine and
   egg.
4 Beat well and place on top of the meat in a suitable dish. Smooth the top
   of the potato and cook, uncovered, for 10–15 min.
5 Sprinkle with a little grated nutmeg or paprika before serving.

Variation
450g (1lb) fresh meat may be used in the recipe instead of cooked meat. At
stage 2 above, cook the fresh meat with the onion etc in the stock for 15 min.
Stir 2–3 times throughout and break down any lumps with a fork. Thicken
with 15g (½oz) wholewheat flour, then finish the dish as above.

Tandoori chicken *(serves 4)*
POWER LEVEL: 100% (FULL)

1 Cut the chicken legs into 2 pieces and the breasts into 4. Cut slits on each side of the chicken pieces well through the flesh to the bone.
2 Place the chicken on plates or a large platter and sprinkle with the salt and lemon juice, rubbing the latter into the flesh on both sides of the pieces, particularly in the slits. Leave to stand for 20–30 min.
3 Mix together the yoghurt, onion, garlic, ginger, chilli and garam masala. If preferred, the mixture may be puréed in a blender or food processor.
4 Drain any lemon juice from the chicken into the marinade. Place in the chicken, turn the pieces over and rub the marinade well into the cuts in the flesh. Cover and refrigerate for at least 24 hr.
5 Remove the chicken from the marinade, shaking off as much of the liquid as possible. Arrange the pieces in a single layer in a shallow dish.
6 Cover and cook for 7 min, turn the pieces over and rearrange them in the dish. Cook, uncovered, for a further 7 min.
7 Test the chicken with a skewer and, if not quite done, either cook for a further 1–2 min or cover and leave to stand for 5 min.
8 Serve on a bed of shredded lettuce, garnished with lemon wedges.

900g (2lb) chicken portions, legs or breasts, skinned
1 × 5ml tsp (1tsp) salt
1 lemon, juice
425ml (¾pt) natural yoghurt
1 small onion, minced or finely chopped
1 clove garlic, crushed
2.5cm (1in) cube fresh ginger, peeled and minced or finely chopped
½ fresh green chilli, minced or finely chopped
2 × 5ml tsp (2tsp) garam masala
for garnish: shredded lettuce and lemon wedges

Pheasant and chicken terrine *(serves 8)*   *colour page 7*
POWER LEVEL: 60%

1 Line a 17.5cm (7in) microwave ring mould or round dish with the rashers of bacon, leaving the ends of the rashers to fold over the top of the filled mould.
2 Finely mince together the pheasant meat, chicken, onion, garlic and belly pork. Add all the remaining ingredients except the garnish and mix well.
3 Carefully spoon the mixture into the prepared dish. Fold the ends of the bacon over the filling, adding extra bacon pieces if necessary to enclose the terrine.
4 Cook at 60% setting for 20–25 min or until the juices run clear when a skewer is inserted into the terrine. Place a plate over the mould and press under a heavy weight in the refrigerator overnight.
5 Turn out onto a serving platter and garnish with orange butterflies and sprigs of parsley. Serve as a starter.

350–450g (¾–1lb) streaky bacon, de-rinded
1 small pheasant, weighing about 900g (2lb), boned
225g (8oz) chicken breast
2 onions
2 cloves garlic, crushed
100g (4oz) belly pork
1 orange, grated rind
salt and black pepper
½ × 5ml tsp (½tsp) ground mace
1 × 15ml tbsp (1tbsp) chopped parsley
6 × 15ml tbsp (6tbsp) red wine
for garnish: orange butterflies and parsley sprigs

Pressed tongue *(serves 8–10)*   *colour page 7*
POWER LEVEL: 100% (FULL) AND 50%

1 Soak the tongue in cold water for 5–6 hr then drain. Place it in a casserole dish which is just a little too large for it—if necessary tie it with string to give a round shape to ensure even cooking results.
2 Add boiling water to cover, the bay leaf, peppercorns and sliced onion. Cover and cook for 10 min on 100% (full) and a further 60–70 min on 50% setting, or until the tongue is tender.
3 Reserve the cooking liquid and plunge the tongue into cold water. When it has cooled sufficiently to handle, carefully remove the skin and cut away any bone and gristle.
4 Place the tongue into a small round dish or tin, approximately 12.5–15cm (5–6in) in diameter. Pour a little of the reserved cooking liquid around the meat then place a plate over the dish.
5 Place a heavy weight on the plate to press the meat. Leave until cold, then chill in the refrigerator. Serve cut into thin slices.

1 salted ox tongue, weighing approximately 1½kg (3lb)
water
boiling water
1 bay leaf
6 peppercorns
1 onion, sliced

675g (1½lb) venison, diced
marinade (see below)
100g (4oz) dried chestnuts
boiling water
2 onions, chopped
4 sticks celery, chopped
1 clove garlic, crushed
40g (1½oz) wholewheat flour
425ml (¾pt) red wine
2 × 15ml tbsp (2tbsp) tomato
  paste
salt and freshly ground black
  pepper
2 bay leaves
6 juniper berries
6 peppercorns, green or black
1 × 15ml tbsp (1tbsp) dark
  demerara sugar
for garnish: chopped parsley

Venison with celery and chestnuts *(serves 6)*   *colour opposite*
POWER LEVEL: 100% (FULL) AND 30%

The venison is marinated for 8 hr before cooking

1 Marinate the venison in the marinade for 8 hr or overnight. Remove the venison and pat dry with kitchen paper towel.
2 Place the chestnuts in a bowl, cover with boiling water and cover the bowl with a lid or pierced clingfilm. Heat for 5 min, allow to stand for 1 hr.
3 Cook the onion, celery and garlic in a covered casserole dish for 6–8 min, stirring once during cooking. Add the venison and cook for a further 4–6 min, stirring once throughout.
4 Stir the flour into the casserole. Gradually add the wine and tomato paste and mix well together. Heat for 5–6 min, uncovered, until boiling, stirring every minute.
5 Season the dish, add the bay leaves, juniper berries and peppercorns. Reduce to 30% setting and cook, covered, for 45 min.
6 Drain the chestnuts, stir into the casserole and cook for a further 30–45 min until the venison is tender.
7 Add the sugar and adjust the seasoning. Serve hot sprinkled with chopped parsley.

675g (1½lb) venison, diced
marinade (see below)
225g (8oz) wholewheat flour
2 × 5ml tsp (2tsp) baking
  powder
½ × 5ml tsp (½tsp) salt
1 × 5ml tsp (1tsp) caraway
  seeds
100g (4oz) suet, grated
water to mix
1 onion, finely chopped
100g (4oz) mushrooms, sliced

Marinade for venison
½ large onion, sliced
6 juniper berries
6 peppercorns, green or black
1 bay leaf
2 × 15ml tbsp (2tbsp) olive oil
2 × 15ml tbsp (2tbsp) wine
  vinegar
200–275ml (⅓–½pt) red wine

Venison and mushroom pudding *(serves 6)*
POWER LEVEL: 100% (FULL) AND 30%

The venison is marinated for 8 hr before cooking

1 Marinate the venison for 8 hr or overnight. Drain from the marinade and reserve the liquid.
2 Place the flour, baking powder, salt, caraway seeds and suet in a bowl. Add sufficient water to give a soft manageable dough, then turn onto a floured board or surface and knead lightly.
3 Roll out two-thirds of the dough and use to line a lightly oiled 825ml (1½pt) pudding basin. Roll out the remaining dough into a circle just large enough to cover the pudding.
4 Cook the onion in a small covered dish for 2–3 min. Mix with the venison and mushrooms and use to fill the lined pudding basin. Dampen the edges of the pastry lid, cover the pudding, and seal the edges well. Make a slit in the lid.
5 Cover the basin with pierced clingfilm and place on a plate. Cook on 30% setting for 45 min. Remove the clingfilm and pour some of the marinade into the pudding through the slit in the lid, to moisten the meat. Re-cover with clingfilm and continue to cook for a further 15–30 min.
6 Serve the pudding from the basin, wrapped in a clean linen napkin.

Variation
This pudding may also be made using cooked venison. Cook the venison in the marinade with the mushrooms for 10 min on 100% (full) setting then a further 1 hr on 30% setting. Alow to cool. Make up the pastry and line the pudding basin as above. Fill with the cooled venison and finish the pudding as before, finally covering with clingfilm.
Cook for 15–18 min on 100% (full), covering the top of the pudding with a circle of aluminium foil after the first 10 min to protect the top from over-cooking. Allow to stand for 10 min before serving as above.

*Venison with Celery and Chestnuts
(above); Prawns with Aubergines
(page 48); Parsnips with Honey and
Dill (page 97)*

Pasta and Pulses

Pasta and pulses cook extremely well in the microwave cooker, requiring very little or no attention during the cooking time and the kitchen remains relatively free of steam. As both pasta and pulses rely mainly on the absorption of water to soften and cook, microwave cooking times are not much shorter than conventional ones, but the results are well worthwhile.

There is now a wide variety of wholewheat pasta available in both supermarkets and healthfood shops, although lasagne and spaghetti are probably the most popular. Pulses—dried beans, peas and lentils—come in many shapes, sizes and colours with over twenty different types from which to choose; the most popular are now easily available in most high street supermarkets as well as wholefood stores. A selection of both pasta and pulses in the store cupboard provides the wholefooder with an excellent supply of convenience foods and the microwave cook with a wealth of available ingredients to serve on their own or as a part of a composite dish.

Pasta

Pasta should be cooked in a large, covered container with plenty of boiling, salted water and a little oil to avoid sticking. When cooking quantities larger than 450g (1lb), you may find that conventional cooking methods are more convenient. When cooking pasta in the microwave, ensure that it is completely covered with water—any pieces that protrude above will become hard and brittle. To help prevent this, hold the pasta under the boiling water with a spoon or fork until it softens, before covering and placing in the microwave to cook. It may be boiled until it is completely cooked in the microwave or the pasta can be cooked for half the recommended time and then allowed to stand for 10 min to soften before draining.

Pulses

With the exception of lentils, all other pulses require soaking before cooking conventionally or by microwave. They should be soaked for at least 5 hr, or overnight, in cold water. Alternatively, cover them with boiling water, cover

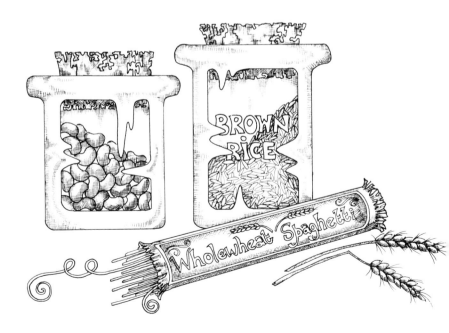

the dish with a lid or pierced clingfilm, and heat in the microwave on 100% (full) for 5 min. Allow them to stand for 1½ hr to swell and soften before draining and rinsing well.

To cook, place the pulses in a large container, ensuring that there is sufficient room for the water to boil during the cooking time. Cover with boiling water from the kettle and bring the dish to the boil in the microwave. Do not add any salt to the water as this prevents the pulses from softening and therefore lengthens the cooking time. The pulses are cooked on 100% (full) setting for the first 10 min, then reduced to 50% setting for the remainder of the cooking time. All pulses should be covered during the cooking period, and be prepared to top up the cooking liquid with extra boiling water from the kettle if necessary.

Pasta and pulses cooking chart

Pasta/Pulse	Cooking
lasagne 225g (8oz)	add pinch of salt, 1 × 15ml tbsp (1tbsp) oil and at least 1.1 litre (2pt) boiling water. Cook 10 min on 100% (full), stand for 2 min
macaroni 225g (8oz)	add pinch of salt, 1 × 15ml tbsp (1tbsp) oil and at least 550ml (1pt) boiling water. Cook 8 min on 100% (full), stand for 3 min
pasta shells 225g (8oz)	add pinch of salt, 1 × 15ml tbsp (1tbsp) oil and at least 825ml (1½pt) boiling water. Cook 15–18 min on 100% (full), stand for 2 min
spaghetti 225g (8oz)	add pinch of salt, 1 × 15ml tbsp (1tbsp) oil and at least 825ml (1½pt) boiling water. Cook 12 min on 100% (full), stand for 2 min
tagliatelle 225g (8oz)	add pinch of salt, 1 × 15ml tbsp (1tbsp) oil and at least 550ml (1pt) boiling water. Cook 5–6 min on 100% (full), stand for 3 min
red lentils 225g (8oz)	cover with boiling water and cook for 15–20 min on 100% (full)
large pulses eg butter beans, flageolets, pinto and kidney beans 225g (8oz), soaked	cover with fresh boiling water. Cook for 10 min on 100% (full) and a further 20–25 min on 50%
small pulses eg aduki, brown or green lentils, black-eye beans 225g (8oz), soaked	cover with fresh boiling water. Cook for 10 min on 100% (full) and a further 10–15 min on 50%
split peas 225g (8oz), soaked	cover with fresh boiling water and cook for 10 min on 100% (full)

225g (8oz) french or runner
   beans
salt
3 × 15ml tbsp (3tbsp) water
100g (4oz) wholewheat
   macaroni
1 × 15ml tbsp (1tbsp)
   sunflower oil
boiling water
1 onion, thinly sliced
1 red pepper, deseeded and
   chopped
75g (3oz) black olives
freshly ground black pepper
for serving: green salad or
   tomato and onion salad

Hot macaroni and green bean salad *(serves 4)*   *colour opposite*
POWER LEVEL: 100% (FULL)

1 Wash and top and tail the beans, cut into 20mm (¾in) lengths. Place in a small covered dish with a pinch of salt and 3 × 15ml tbsp (3tbsp) water. Cook for 4–5 min until just tender, stirring once during cooking.
2 Cook the macaroni in a large covered dish with a little salt, oil and plenty of boiling water to cover for 8 min. Allow to stand for 3 min, then drain.
3 Place the onion and red pepper in a bowl, cover and cook for 4 min, stirring once throughout. Add the olives, the drained green beans and the macaroni. Mix together well and season with salt and ground black pepper to taste.
4 Reheat for 3–4 min, uncovered, until piping hot, stirring once. Serve immediately with a green, or a tomato and onion, salad.

1 × 15ml tbsp (1tbsp) olive oil
450g (1lb) courgettes, trimmed
   and cut into 12mm (½in)
   slices
225g (8oz) wholewheat
   tagliatelle
salt
1 × 15ml tbsp (1tbsp)
   sunflower oil
boiling water
freshly ground black pepper
40g (1½oz) parmesan cheese,
   grated
for garnish: paprika and grated
   parmesan cheese, optional

Tagliatelle with fried courgettes *(serves 3–4)*   *colour opposite*
POWER LEVEL: 100% (FULL)

1 Heat a large browning dish in the microwave for 5 min. Add the olive oil and prepared courgettes. Cover the dish with kitchen paper towel and cook for 3 min. Turn the courgettes over and cook for a further 3 min. Leave the courgettes in the browning dish to keep warm.
2 Cook the tagliatelle in a large dish or bowl with a little salt, the sunflower oil and plenty of boiling water to cover. Cover the dish with a lid or pierced clingfilm and cook for 5 min. Leave to stand for 3 min.
3 Drain the tagliatelle and mix with the courgettes in a serving dish. Season well and stir in the parmesan cheese.
4 Heat for 2–3 min until piping hot. Allow to stand for 2 min before garnishing with paprika and a little extra grated parmesan cheese. Serve immediately.

225g (8oz) wholewheat
   spaghetti
salt
1 × 15ml tbsp (1tbsp)
   sunflower oil
boiling water
1 large clove garlic, crushed
175g (6oz) mushrooms, sliced
small piece root ginger, peeled
   and grated
pepper
2 spring onions, trimmed and
   sliced
100g (4oz) cabbage, shredded
1 × 15ml tbsp (1tbsp) soy sauce
100g (4oz) cooked pork, cut
   into strips
100g (4oz) peeled prawns
for garnish: chopped parsley

Eastern spaghetti *(serves 4)*   *colour opposite*
POWER LEVEL: 100% (FULL)

1 Cook the spaghetti with a pinch of salt, the oil and plenty of boiling water in a large covered dish, pushing the pasta as it softens into the water. Cook for 12 min, stand for 2 min, then drain and rinse well in cold water.
2 Place the garlic, mushrooms and ginger in a large serving dish. Mix well together, cover and cook for 3 min, stirring once throughout. Add salt and pepper to taste.
3 Add the onions and cabbage, stir in the soy sauce and cook, uncovered, for 4 min, stirring once halfway through.
4 Add the pork and prawns and cook for 2 min. Add the spaghetti and cook for a further 4–6 min, stirring occasionally, until piping hot.
5 Check seasoning and sprinkle with chopped parsley before serving.

Tagliatelle with Fried Courgettes (above); Eastern Spaghetti (above); Hot Macaroni and Green Bean Salad (above)

75g (3oz) dried apricots
cold water
175g (6oz) wholewheat pasta
  shells
good pinch salt
1 × 15ml tbsp (1tbsp)
  sunflower oil
boiling water
25g (1oz) sunflower margarine
1 onion, chopped
1 red pepper, deseeded and
  chopped
25g (1oz) wholewheat flour
425ml (¾pt) boiling vegetable
  stock
1 × 15ml tbsp (1tbsp) chopped
  fresh tarragon or 1 × 5ml tsp
  (1tsp) dried tarragon
salt and pepper
350g (12oz) cooked chicken,
  diced
for serving: green vegetables or
  salad

Chicken and apricot pasta *(serves 4–6)*
POWER LEVEL: 100% (FULL)

1   Cover the apricots with cold water in a small dish. Cover the dish and heat for 5 min, then leave to stand for at least 10 min.
2   Cook the pasta shells with a good pinch of salt, the oil and plenty of boiling water in a large covered dish for 10–12 min. Allow to stand for 3 min, then drain and rinse in cold water.
3   Melt the margarine in a large serving dish for 1 min, add the onion and pepper, cover and cook for 3 min, stirring once. Add the flour and stir well.
4   Add the boiling stock gradually, stirring well after each addition and cook, uncovered, for 4–5 min, stirring every minute until thick.
5   Roughly chop the apricots and add to the sauce with the tarragon, salt and pepper. Cover and cook for 4 min. Stir in the chicken and pasta.
6   Cook, uncovered, for 4 min, stirring occasionally, until hot through. Adjust seasoning to taste and serve with green vegetables or salad.

675g (1½lb) tomatoes,
  skinned, deseeded and diced
4–6 cloves garlic, crushed
1–2 × 15ml tbsp (1–2tbsp)
  chopped fresh basil or
  1–2 × 5ml tsp (1–2tsp) dried
  basil
2 × 15ml tbsp (2tbsp) olive or
  sunflower oil
225g (8oz) wholewheat
  spaghetti
pinch salt
1 × 15ml tbsp (1tbsp)
  sunflower oil
boiling water
salt and freshly ground black
  pepper

Spaghetti in tomato sauce *(serves 4)*
POWER LEVEL: 100% (FULL)

1   Mix together the tomatoes, garlic, basil and 2 × 15ml tbsp (2tbsp) olive or sunflower oil and leave to stand while the spaghetti is cooking.
2   Place the spaghetti in a large bowl or shallow dish with the salt and 1 × 15ml tbsp (1tbsp) sunflower oil. Cover with boiling water and push the spaghetti down into the water as it softens. Cover with a lid or pierced clingfilm and cook for 12 min. Stand for 2 min, then drain.
3   Add the spaghetti to the tomato sauce and toss well. Season and serve immediately.

Pasta florentine *(serves 4)*

POWER LEVEL: 100% (FULL)
CONVENTIONAL OVEN TEMPERATURE: 200°C (400°F) MARK 6

225g (8oz) wholewheat pasta
  shells
pinch salt
1 × 15ml tbsp (1tbsp) oil
boiling water
675g (1½lb) spinach, trimmed
  and washed
4 eggs
100g (4oz) farmhouse cheddar
  cheese, grated
salt and pepper

1 Place the pasta in a large bowl, add the salt and oil. Pour on plenty of boiling water to cover the pasta. Cover the bowl and cook for 12 min. Allow to stand for 2 min.
2 Drain and rinse the pasta and arrange it around the outside of an oven-proof dish.
3 Cook the spinach in a large covered dish for 12 min, stirring once or twice throughout. Drain and coarsely chop. Arrange the spinach in a ring inside the pasta shells.
4 Beat the eggs in a bowl, add the grated cheese and seasoning. Pour the mixture into the centre of the dish and cook in the conventional preheated oven for 15–20 min until just set.
5 Serve immediately.

DO NOT FREEZE

Butter bean bourguignon *(serves 4–5)*   *colour page 11*

POWER LEVEL: 100% (FULL) AND 50%

225g (8oz) butter beans, soaked
boiling water
100g (4oz) bacon, chopped
1 large onion, chopped
1 clove garlic, crushed
450g (1lb) tomatoes, skinned
  and sliced
salt and pepper
1 bay leaf
1 × 5ml tsp (1tsp) mixed herbs
275ml (½pt) red wine
2 × 15ml tbsp (2tbsp) tomato
  paste
100g (4oz) mushrooms, sliced
for serving: green vegetables or a
  mixed salad

1 Drain and rinse the beans and place in a large bowl. Cover with boiling water, then cover the dish with a lid or pierced clingfilm. Cook for 10 min on 100% (full) setting, then leave to stand.
2 Cook the bacon in a covered dish for 2 min. Add the onion and garlic and cook, covered, for 3 min, stirring once.
3 Add the tomatoes, seasoning, herbs, wine and tomato paste. Mix well, cover and cook for 10 min on 100% (full) stirring once throughout.
4 Drain the butter beans and stir into the dish. Cover and cook for 10 min on 100% (full) and a further 20 min on 50%, or until tender.
5 Add the mushrooms and continue to cook for a further 5 min. Correct the seasoning and serve immediately with green vegetables or a mixed salad.

Macaroni with soured cream and herbs *(serves 3–4)*

POWER LEVEL: 100% (FULL)

225g (8oz) wholewheat
  macaroni
pinch salt
1 × 15ml tbsp (1tbsp)
  sunflower oil
boiling water
150ml (¼pt) soured cream
1 × 15ml tbsp (1tbsp) each
  chopped fresh parsley, chives
  and rosemary or 1 × 15ml
  tbsp (1tbsp) dried mixed
  herbs
2 cloves garlic, crushed
salt and freshly ground black
  pepper
grated parmesan cheese to
  taste

1 Cook the macaroni in a large covered dish with a pinch of salt, the oil and plenty of boiling water for 8 min. Allow to stand for 3 min, then drain.
2 Warm the cream in a bowl for 1–1½ min. Add the herbs and garlic and season to taste. Add the macaroni and toss well in the cream.
3 Serve on individual warmed plates, sprinkled liberally with grated parmesan cheese.

DO NOT FREEZE

225g (8oz) split peas, soaked
boiling water
3 × 15ml tbsp (3tbsp) olive oil
1 lemon, grated rind and juice
1 clove garlic, crushed
1 green chilli, deseeded and
finely chopped
1 × 5ml tsp (1tsp) salt,
approximately
freshly ground black pepper
for serving: crusty bread or
crudités

Spiced split pea dip *(serves 6–8)*   *colour opposite*
POWER LEVEL: 100% (FULL)

This makes a very refreshing alternative to hummus, and the lemon gives a refreshing tang. Serve as a starter or snack

1   Drain and rinse the peas, place them in a bowl and cover with boiling water. Cover the bowl and cook for 8–10 min, until soft. Drain.
2   Place the peas in a blender or food processor and purée with the oil, lemon rind and juice. Add extra lemon juice or water if necessary to give a soft consistency.
3   Add remaining ingredients, mix well and adjust the seasoning.
4   Serve as a dip with crusty bread or crudités.

225g (8oz) chick peas, soaked
450g (1lb) pumpkin
salt
2 onions, chopped
1 small green pepper, deseeded
and chopped
1 clove garlic, crushed
1 bay leaf
pinch cayenne pepper
½ × 5ml tsp (½tsp) chilli
powder
4 cloves
freshly ground black pepper
425ml (¾pt) boiling vegetable
stock
for garnish: chopped parsley

Chick peas with pumpkin *(serves 4)*
POWER LEVEL: 100% (FULL) AND 50%

1   Drain and rinse the chick peas. Peel and deseed the pumpkin and cut the flesh into 6–12mm (¼–½in) dice. Place in a bowl or sieve and sprinkle generously with salt. Leave to stand.
2   Cook the onion, green pepper and garlic in a large covered bowl for 3–4 min, stirring once throughout. Add the drained chick peas, bay leaf, spices, salt and freshly ground black pepper and stock. Cover and cook for 10 min on 100% (full), then a further 20 min on 50% until the chick peas are tender.
3   Rinse the pumpkin well and add to the chick peas. Cover and cook for 6–8 min on 100% (full) setting until the pumpkin is cooked, stirring once. Correct the seasoning and serve garnished with chopped parsley.

50g (2oz) red kidney beans,
soaked
boiling water
175g (6oz) wholewheat flour
pinch salt
75g (3oz) butter or vegetable
margarine
tepid water to mix
1 small onion, chopped
100g (4oz) curd cheese
150ml (¼pt) soured cream
2 eggs
50g (2oz) farmhouse cheddar
cheese, grated
salt and pepper
paprika for sprinkling
for serving: mixed salad

Kidney bean quiche *(serves 6)*   *colour opposite*
POWER LEVEL: 100% (FULL) AND 50%

1   Drain and rinse the beans. Place in a bowl and cover with boiling water. Cover with a lid or pierced clingfilm and cook for 10 min on 100% (full) and a further 10–15 min on 50%, or until tender.
2   Place the flour and pinch of salt for the pastry in a bowl and rub in the butter or vegetable margarine until it resembles fine breadcrumbs.
3   Add sufficient tepid water to bind, then turn onto a floured board and knead lightly. Roll out to a circle and line a 20cm (8in) flan dish.
4   Place small strips of foil around the upright edges of the pastry and prick the base with a fork. Line the pastry case with pieces of kitchen paper towel and fill with baking beans. Cook for 4 min on 100% (full), remove the beans, paper and foil and cook for a further 1½–2 min.
5   Cook the onion in a small covered dish for 2 min. Stir in the kidney beans and place in the pastry case.
6   Whisk together the curd cheese, cream and eggs. Add the cheddar cheese and season to taste. Pour the filling into the flan case.
7   Sprinkle the flan with paprika pepper and cook for 15 min on 50% setting or until set. Allow to stand for 10 min before serving hot or cold with salad.

Spiced Split Pea Dip (above);
Kidney Bean Quiche (above)

1 large onion, chopped
1–2 cloves garlic, crushed
1 red pepper, deseeded and chopped
450g (1lb) tomatoes, peeled and chopped
225g (8oz) courgettes, trimmed and diced
salt and pepper
1 × 5ml tsp (1tsp) dried basil
225g (8oz) mushrooms, sliced
40g (1½oz) sunflower margarine
40g (1½oz) wholewheat flour
275ml (½pt) milk
150ml (¼pt) natural yoghurt
75g (3oz) farmhouse cheddar cheese, grated
25g (1oz) parmesan cheese, grated
225g (8oz) wholewheat lasagne
pinch salt
1 × 15ml tbsp (1tbsp) sunflower oil
boiling water
parmesan cheese, grated, for sprinkling

Vegetable lasagne (serves 5–6)
POWER LEVEL: 100% (FULL) AND 70%

1 Place the onion and garlic in a bowl, cover with a lid or pierced clingfilm, cook for 2 min on 100% (full), stir and cook for a further 2 min. Add the red pepper, cook for a further 2 min.
2 Add the tomatoes, courgettes, seasoning and basil. Cover and cook for 10 min, stirring once. Add the mushrooms and cook for 5 min, uncovered. Cover the dish to keep warm.
3 Melt the margarine in a bowl or jug for 1 min. Add the flour and stir well. Add the milk gradually, stirring well after each addition. Cook for 4–5 min, stirring every minute until thick. Add the yoghurt and cheeses, mix well together and correct the seasoning.
4 Place the lasagne in a large dish or bowl with the salt and oil. Add plenty of boiling water, cover and cook for 2 min then leave to stand for 2 min.
5 Arrange the vegetables and lasagne in alternate layers in a large serving dish, starting with a layer of vegetables and finishing with a layer of lasagne. (The lasagne is easy to handle if lifted straight from the dish it was cooked in with a draining spoon.)
6 Top the lasagne with the cheese sauce. Heat the complete dish on 70% setting for 6–8 min until heated through. Serve sprinkled with a little extra grated parmesan cheese.

175g (6oz) flageolet beans
boiling water
25g (1oz) sunflower margarine
1 small onion, chopped
100g (4oz) mushrooms, sliced
450g (1lb) thick cod fillet, skinned and cut into strips
1 × 15ml tbsp (1tbsp) fresh dill or 1 × 5ml tsp (1tsp) dried dill
salt and pepper
150ml (¼pt) natural yoghurt
2 bananas, sliced
1 lemon, juice and grated rind

Flageolets with cod (serves 4–5)   colour page 107
POWER LEVEL: 100% (FULL) AND 50%

1 Drain and rinse the beans. Cover with boiling water and cook, covered, for 10 min on 100% (full) and a further 20–25 min on 50% until tender. Leave covered and allow to stand.
2 Melt the margarine in a large shallow dish for 1 min on 100% (full). Add the onion, mix well, cover and continue to cook for 3 min. Stir in the mushrooms, cod and dill and cook, uncovered, for 7–8 min, stirring gently once throughout. Add salt and pepper to taste.
3 Drain the beans and add to the dish, cook for 2 min. Add the yoghurt and heat for a further 2 min.
4 Brush the banana slices with the lemon juice and stir into the dish. Adjust the seasoning, and garnish with the grated lemon rind before serving.

225g (8oz) black-eye beans, soaked
550ml (1pt) boiling stock
450g (1lb) tomatoes, skinned and chopped
100g (4oz) long-grain brown rice
salt and pepper
pinch cayenne pepper
2 × 15ml tbsp (2tbsp) chopped parsley

'Hoppin' John' (serves 4)
POWER LEVEL: 100% (FULL) AND 50%

This substantial dish originated in the southern states of the USA

1 Drain and rinse the beans. Place in a large bowl or dish with the boiling stock, cover and cook for 10 min on 100% (full) and a further 10 min on 50%, or until the beans are just tender.
2 Add the tomatoes and rice and cook, covered, on 100% (full) for 15–20 min until the rice is tender. Allow to stand for 5 min.
3 Season the dish, and stir in the chopped parsley before serving.

Grains and Nuts

Grains are simple to cook, versatile, nutritious, and provide the wholefooder with an extremely satisfying, value-for-money ingredient, while nuts are a major source of protein and high-energy food. The two together make an excellent combination, and a good basis for improvisation for the microwave cook.

Whether grains are whole, cracked, flaked or ground, they depend on the absorption of water or stock to become plump and tender. The main advantage of cooking them in the microwave is that very little attention is required, and the kitchen remains relatively free of steam. Probably the best known of all the grains is rice, and brown rice, with its nutty texture and delicious flavour, contains valuable nutrients in the outer husk—the part which is removed from the refined white variety.

Cooking

Make sure that the container is large enough for the water to boil and to allow for the expansion of the grains during cooking; the dishes should be covered with a lid or pierced clingfilm during the heating or cooking period. Carefully measure the amount of water or stock so that the grains will absorb all the liquid, thereby retaining more B vitamins. The chart below gives the approximate quantity of liquid the grains absorb, together with cooking times, although these will vary depending on whether the recipe requires a lower power setting because of the addition of other ingredients. It is unlikely that grains will be cooked and served on their own—with the exception of brown rice—therefore the chart is intended as a guide when converting your own grain recipes to cook by microwave.

Grain cooking chart

Grain	Ratio liquid to grain	Approximate cooking time 100% (full)
barley	2–2½:1	35–40 min
brown rice	2:1	20–25 min
buckwheat	2:1	10–15 min
millet	3:1	10–15 min
rye	2:1	35–40 min
wheat	2:1	35–40 min

Rye cooked with raisins (serves 4)
POWER LEVEL: 100% (FULL)

Serve this dish as an alternative to rice

225g (8oz) rye groats or grain
75g (3oz) raisins
50g (2oz) bacon, de-rinded and diced
½ × 5ml tsp (½tsp) salt
550ml (1pt) boiling vegetable stock

1 Place the rye groats or grain, raisins, bacon and salt in a large bowl or casserole dish. Stir in the vegetable stock and mix well.
2 Cover and cook for 35–40 min until the rye is soft, stirring once or twice during the cooking time.
3 Allow to stand for 5 min before serving as an alternative to rice.

225g (8oz) long-grain brown
 rice
550ml (1pt) boiling vegetable
 stock
pinch salt
1 large onion, chopped
75g (3oz) button mushrooms,
 sliced
1 × 15ml tbsp (1tbsp) tamari
 sauce
salt and pepper
4 hard-boiled eggs
50g (2oz) peanuts
175g (6oz) beanshoots
for garnish: chopped fresh
 coriander leaves
for serving: salad

Peanut and beanshoot risotto *(serves 4)*   *colour opposite*
POWER LEVEL: 100% (FULL)

1 Place the rice in a large bowl with the stock and salt. Cover and cook for 20–25 min, allow to stand for 5 min.
2 In a large shallow serving dish cook the onion, covered, for 2 min. Add the rice, mushrooms, tamari sauce and salt and pepper to taste. Cover and cook for 4 min, stirring once throughout.
3 Chop three of the hard-boiled eggs and cut the remaining one into quarters. Add the chopped eggs to the risotto with the peanuts and beanshoots. Cook, uncovered, for 4–5 min until hot through, stirring every minute.
4 Garnish with the egg quarters and chopped coriander leaves. Serve hot with a salad.

DO NOT FREEZE

100g (4oz) burghul (cracked
 wheat)
cold water
2 sticks celery, finely sliced
4 spring onions, trimmed and
 finely sliced
½ red pepper, deseeded and
 diced
½ green pepper, deseeded and
 diced
1 sprig mint, chopped
2 × 15ml tbsp (2tbsp) clear
 honey
2 × 15ml tbsp (2tbsp) lemon
 juice
2 × 15ml tbsp (2tbsp) olive oil
salt and pepper

Cracked wheat salad with honey dressing *(serves 4)*
POWER LEVEL: 100% (FULL)   *colour opposite*

1 Soak the burghul in cold water for approximately 1 hr until it has swollen.
2 While the burghul is soaking, cook the celery, onion and peppers in a small covered dish for 4 min, stirring once during cooking. Leave to cool.
3 Drain the burghul and wring it dry in a clean tea-towel. Mix the grain with the cooled vegetables and add the chopped mint.
4 Whisk the honey, lemon juice, oil and salt and pepper to taste together thoroughly, or alternatively place the ingredients in a small screw-top jar and shake vigorously to blend the dressing.
5 Toss the cracked wheat salad in the dressing just before serving.

DO NOT FREEZE

450g (1lb) mushrooms, sliced
50g (2oz) bacon, de-rinded and
 diced
1 onion, chopped
2 cloves garlic, crushed
boiling water
225g (8oz) millet
salt and pepper
1 × 15ml tbsp (1tbsp) chopped
 chives

Millet and Mushroom Hash (above);
Cracked Wheat Salad with Honey
Dressing (above); Peanut and
Beanshoot Risotto (above)

Millet and mushroom hash *(serves 4)*   *colour opposite*
POWER LEVEL: 100% (FULL) AND 50%
CONVENTIONAL OVEN TEMPERATURE: 180°C (350°F) MARK 4

1 Mix together the mushrooms, bacon, onion and garlic. Place in a large bowl, cover and cook for 8–10 min on 100% (full) setting, stirring once throughout.
2 Boil a kettle of water and place 275ml (½pt) into a large bowl or dish. Use the remainder of the boiling water to wash the millet in a sieve.
3 Add the washed millet to the water in the bowl or dish, cover and cook for 5 min on 100% (full) setting and a further 10 min on 50%.
4 Mix together the millet and the mushroom mixture. Season well and add the chopped chives.
5 Lightly grease a 20cm (8in) flan dish and press the millet mixture into it. Cook in a preheated oven for 1–1¼ hr until crisp. Serve hot.

225g (8oz) long-grain brown
  rice
pinch salt
550ml (1pt) boiling vegetable
  stock
1 large onion, quartered and
  finely sliced
2 cloves garlic, crushed
1 large courgette, trimmed
  and finely sliced
1 aubergine, trimmed, halved
  and sliced
1 green chilli, deseeded and
  finely chopped
1 bay leaf
6 cloves
6 peppercorns
1 cinnamon stick
1 × 5ml tsp (1tsp) turmeric
2 × 5ml tsp (2tsp) ground
  cumin
½ × 5ml tsp (½tsp) chilli
  powder
salt to taste
2 tomatoes, sliced
100g (4oz) mushrooms, sliced
for garnish: chopped parsley or
  coriander

Curried vegetable rice *(serves 3–4)*   *colour page 87*
POWER LEVEL: 100% (FULL)

1 Cook the rice in a covered dish with the pinch of salt and stock for 20–25 min. Allow to stand.
2 Mix together the onion, garlic, courgette, aubergine, chilli, bay leaf and spices in a large dish. Cover and cook for 10–12 min until soft, stirring once or twice throughout. Add salt to taste.
3 Add the rice, tomatoes and mushrooms to the vegetables. Stir well and heat, uncovered, for 5 min, stirring occasionally until hot through. Serve immediately garnished with parsley or coriander.

175g (6oz) pot barley
boiling water
1 large onion, chopped
2 carrots, sliced
2 courgettes, trimmed and
  sliced
175g (6oz) swede, diced
1 red pepper, deseeded and
  roughly chopped
550ml (1pt) boiling vegetable
  stock
2 × 15ml tbsp (2tbsp) tomato
  paste
salt and pepper
1 bay leaf
1 × 5ml tsp (1tsp) fresh
  chopped basil or ½ × 5ml
  tsp (½tsp) dried basil
for garnish: a little extra fresh
  chopped or dried basil

Barley pot *(serves 4–6)*
POWER LEVEL: 100% (FULL)

1 Place the barley in a bowl or dish, cover with boiling water and leave to soak while preparing the vegetables.
2 Place the onion, carrots, courgettes and swede in a large casserole dish, cover and cook for 6 min, stirring once halfway through. Add the red pepper.
3 Drain the barley and add to the vegetables with the stock, tomato paste, seasoning, bay leaf and basil.
4 Cover and cook for 35–40 min until the barley is tender. Adjust the seasoning and serve garnished with a sprinkling of basil.

Maizemeal balls with walnut sauce (serves 4)
POWER LEVEL: 100% (FULL) AND 70%

1 Stir the maize meal, salt and paprika into the boiling water and mix well together. Cook, uncovered, for 2 min, stir and continue to cook for a further 1–2 min until thick. Allow to cool.
2 Form the cooled maize meal into balls, using about 1 × 15ml tbsp (1tbsp) for each one. Arrange the balls in a serving dish.
3 Place the walnuts in a food processor or blender and chop finely with the oil and garlic. Turn the nuts into a dish and add the dill, vinegar, stock and salt and pepper to taste. Stir well.
4 Pour the walnut sauce over the maizemeal balls. Cover and heat for 5–6 min on 70% until hot through.
5 Allow to stand for a few minutes before serving hot.

150g (5oz) maize meal
½ × 5ml tsp (½tsp) salt
2 × 5ml tsp (2tsp) paprika
550ml (1pt) boiling water
200g (7oz) walnuts
2 × 15ml tbsp (2tbsp) olive oil
2 cloves garlic, crushed
1 × 5ml tsp (1tsp) dill weed
2 × 15ml tbsp (2tbsp) wine vinegar
275ml (½pt) boiling vegetable stock
salt and pepper

Cashew and walnut cutlets (serves 4)   colour page 11
POWER LEVEL: 100% (FULL)

The cutlets are cooked in a browning dish

1 Place all the ingredients except the oil in a bowl and mix well together.
2 Divide the mixture into 8 and shape each piece into a round or wedge. Cover and chill in the refrigerator for at least 1 hr.
3 Preheat a large browning dish for 5 min. Brush lightly with oil and quickly add the cutlets, placing wedge-shaped ones with the pointed ends towards the centre of the dish.
4 Place the browning dish back into the microwave and cook the cutlets for 2½ min, turn them over and cook for a further 1½–2 min on the second side.
5 Serve hot or cold.

150g (5oz) cashew nuts, finely chopped
75g (3oz) walnuts, finely chopped
50g (2oz) wholewheat breadcrumbs
1 small onion, finely chopped
1 × 15ml tbsp (1tbsp) chopped parsley
salt and freshly ground black pepper
½ × 5ml tsp (½tsp) each turmeric and allspice
1 × 5ml tsp (1tsp) ground cumin
1 large egg, beaten
oil

Tomato and mixed nut quiche (serves 6)
POWER LEVEL: 100% (FULL) AND 30%

1 Place the flour and salt in a mixing bowl. Rub in the fat until the mixture resembles fine breadcrumbs. Add sufficient tepid water to mix, kneading the dough lightly together. Roll out the pastry and line a 20cm (8in) flan dish. Prick the pastry base.
2 Line the sides of the pastry flan with a strip of aluminium foil. Place a layer of kitchen paper in the base of the flan and fill with baking beans. Cook the pastry case for 4 min on 100% (full) setting. Remove the beans, paper and foil and cook for a further 1½–2 min.
3 Arrange the onion in the base of the flan case, add the chopped nuts and cover with a layer of tomato slices. Sprinkle with the basil.
4 Beat together the eggs, milk, yoghurt, salt and pepper and parmesan cheese. Pour the mixture into the flan case.
5 Cook on 30% setting for 18–22 min and allow to stand for 5–10 min. Serve hot or cold.

DO NOT FREEZE

175g (6oz) wholewheat flour
pinch salt
75g (3oz) butter or vegetable margarine
tepid water to mix
1 small onion, finely sliced
100g (4oz) mixed nuts, roughly chopped
2 tomatoes, sliced
1 × 5ml tsp (1tsp) chopped fresh basil or ½ × 5ml tsp (½tsp) dried basil
3 eggs
150ml (¼pt) milk
150ml (¼pt) natural yoghurt
salt and freshly ground black pepper
25g (1oz) parmesan cheese, grated

225g (8oz) dried chestnuts
boiling water
2 × 15ml tbsp (2tbsp)
    sunflower oil
1 leek, trimmed and finely
    sliced
2 sticks celery, sliced
½ green pepper, deseeded and
    diced
small piece fresh ginger, peeled
    and grated
1 bay leaf
pinch nutmeg
25g (1oz) wholewheat flour
425ml (¾pt) boiling vegetable
    stock or 275ml (½pt) boiling
    vegetable stock and 150ml
    (¼pt) red wine
salt and freshly ground black
    pepper
1 × 15ml tbsp (1tbsp) dark
    demerara sugar
2 × 15ml tbsp (2tbsp) tamari
    sauce
for serving: plain boiled rice or
    noodles

Chestnut casserole *(serves 4–6)*   *colour opposite*
POWER LEVEL: 100% (FULL) AND 50%

1   Place the chestnuts in a dish, cover with boiling water. Cover the dish and heat for 5 min on 100% (full) setting. Allow to stand for 1hr, then drain.
2   Heat the oil in a large casserole dish for 2 min. Add the leek, celery, pepper, ginger, bay leaf and nutmeg. Toss over in the oil, cover and cook for 6 min, stirring once during cooking.
3   Stir the flour into the vegetables and gradually add the liquid. Cook, uncovered, for 3–4 min until boiling, stirring every minute. Add the salt and pepper, chestnuts, sugar and tamari sauce.
4   Cover the dish and cook for 20–25 min on 50% setting. Adjust the seasoning before serving with boiled rice or noodles.

1 egg
450g (1lb) buckwheat groats
550ml (1pt) boiling vegetable
    stock
salt and pepper
1 onion, quartered and finely
    sliced
for garnish: chopped parsley

Kasha *(serves 4–6)*
POWER LEVEL: 100% (FULL) AND 50%

Kasha is a traditional russian dish with a delicious nutty flavour

1   Beat the egg in a medium-size casserole dish, add the buckwheat and mix well together.
2   Cook, uncovered, for 2 min and stir with a fork to separate the grains.
3   Add the boiling stock, salt and pepper. Cover and cook on 100% (full) setting for 5 min. Add the onion, stir and cook for a further 5–8 min on 50% setting.
4   Fluff the kasha with a fork, check the seasoning, and sprinkle with chopped parsley before serving.

550ml (1pt) boiling water
4 × 15ml tbsp (4tbsp) medium
    oatmeal
salt
for serving: demerara sugar and
    milk, optional

Oatmeal porridge *(serves 2–3)*
POWER LEVEL: 100% (FULL) AND 50%

This is a traditional scottish porridge, but for more general appeal may be served with demerara sugar and milk

1   Place the boiling water in a large bowl or dish and stir in the oatmeal until blended.
2   Heat for 2–3 min on 100% (full) setting until boiling, stirring every minute.
3   Reduce to 50% setting and cook, uncovered, for 8–10 min, stirring once or twice throughout.
4   Add salt to taste, or serve with demerara sugar and milk if preferred.

Chestnut Casserole (above)

1 onion, chopped
4 medium-size mushrooms,
  sliced
75g (3oz) cooked long-grain
  brown rice (page 77)
salt and pepper
2 × 5ml tsp (2tsp) tamari sauce
4 eggs
2 × 15ml tbsp (2tbsp) milk

Rice omelette *(serves 2)*
POWER LEVEL: 100% (FULL)

The omelette is cooked in the microwave and the top browned under a conventional grill

1 Lightly grease a 20cm (8in) round dish.
2 Place the onion and mushrooms in a bowl or dish, cover and cook for 2–3 min, stirring once halfway through.
3 Stir in the rice, seasoning and tamari sauce, cover and cook for a further 2 min, stirring once.
4 Beat together the eggs and milk with a little seasoning. Pour into the greased dish and cook for 2 min, covered, stirring gently after 1 min. Uncover and cook for a further 30–45 sec.
5 Quickly brown the top of the omelette under a preheated grill. Meanwhile, reheat the rice mixture in the microwave for 1 min.
6 Loosen the base of the omelette from the dish with a palette knife and invert onto a hot serving plate. Spoon the rice filling onto the omelette, fold carefully and serve immediately.

DO NOT FREEZE

100g (4oz) mushrooms, finely
  chopped
1 clove garlic, crushed
225g (8oz) hazelnuts, ground in
  a food processor or blender
salt and freshly ground black
  pepper
½ × 5ml tsp (½tsp) grated
  nutmeg
25g (1oz) wholewheat flour
2 × 15ml tbsp (2tbsp) tomato
  paste
for garnish: sprigs parsley
for serving: fingers of toast
  and/or a salad

Hazelnut pâté *(serves 5–6)*   *colour page 15*
POWER LEVEL: 100% (FULL) AND 60%

1 Place the mushrooms in a dish, cover and cook for 3–4 min on 100% (full) setting, stirring once during cooking.
2 Add all the remaining ingredients except the parsley and mix well together. Divide the mixture between 5–6 well-greased ramekin dishes.
3 Place the dishes in a circle on the microwave cooker shelf and cook, uncovered, for 9–12 min on 60% setting.
4 Allow to cool, then chill in the refrigerator. Garnish each pâté with a small sprig of parsley before serving with fingers of toast and/or a salad.

4 wholewheat pitta breads
peanut butter
1 small onion, finely chopped
1 small eating apple, cored and
  finely diced
75g (3oz) peanuts
225g (8oz) cottage cheese
½ × 5ml tsp (½tsp) paprika
salt and pepper
for serving: mixed salad or
  chutney

Peanut and cottage cheese pittas *(serves 4–6)*
POWER LEVEL: 100% (FULL)

Serve these pittas as a light lunch or snack

1 Cut the pittas into halves and carefully open up each half to form an envelope. Spread a little peanut butter in each piece.
2 Cook the onion in a small covered dish for 3–4 min until soft, stirring once throughout.
3 Add the apple, peanuts, cottage cheese, paprika and salt and pepper to taste. Mix well together.
4 Fill each pitta envelope with the peanut mixture. Place the pitta halves on the microwave cooker shelf with the thin ends of the pittas pointing towards the centre.
5 Heat, uncovered, for 2–3 min until hot through and serve with mixed salad or chutney.

Cheesy semolina cakes (serves 8)

POWER LEVEL: 100% (FULL)

These cakes are cooked in a browning dish in the microwave but alternatively could be deep-fat fried conventionally

1 Heat the milk in a jug for 5–6 min until boiling. Add the salt and semolina and stir well. Cook for 2–3 min, stirring occasionally until thickened.
2 Rinse a china plate in cold water, spread the semolina mixture in a layer 12mm (½in) thick on the cold surface and allow to cool.
3 Cut the semolina into 16 rounds using a biscuit or pastry cutter. Cut a round the same size from each slice of cheese.
4 Use a little of the beaten egg to stick one slice of cheese between 2 semolina rounds. Continue to make 8 cakes.
5 Mix together the breadcrumbs, flour and parsley. Brush each cake with the beaten egg and roll in the breadcrumbs mixture, taking care to seal the sides of the cakes well.
6 Heat a large browning dish for 5 min. Brush the surface lightly with oil and add the semolina cakes quickly. Cook for 2 min, turn the cakes over and continue to cook for a further 1½ min on the second side. Serve hot.

550ml (1pt) milk
pinch salt
100g (4oz) wholewheat
    semolina
8 thin slices cheddar cheese
2 eggs, beaten
50g (2oz) wholewheat
    breadcrumbs
50g (2oz) wholewheat flour
2 × 15ml tbsp (2tbsp) chopped
    parsley or 2 × 5ml tsp (2tsp)
    dried parsley
oil

Bacon and nut ring (serves 4)

POWER LEVEL: 100% (FULL) AND 70%

1 Cook the onion, garlic, bacon and celery in a covered dish for 4 min, stirring once during cooking.
2 Stir in the flour, then gradually add the tomato juice. Cook, uncovered, for 3–4 min, stirring every minute until thickened. Add the remaining ingredients and mix well together.
3 Lightly oil a 17.5cm (7in) microwave ring mould, press the mixture into the dish and smooth the top.
4 Cook for 7–8 min on 70% setting and allow to stand for 2–3 min. Turn out onto a serving plate or dish. Garnish with watercress before serving with tomato sauce.

1 onion, chopped
1 clove garlic, crushed
100g (4oz) bacon, de-rinded
    and chopped
2 sticks celery, chopped
1 × 15ml tbsp (1tbsp)
    wholewheat flour
175ml (6fl oz) tomato juice
100g (4oz) wholewheat
    breadcrumbs
100g (4oz) nuts, chopped
1 × 15ml tbsp (1tbsp) chopped
    parsley
1 × 15ml tbsp (1tbsp) rolled
    oats
1 egg, beaten
salt and pepper
for garnish: watercress
for serving: tomato sauce
    (page 25)

Almond and rice rissoles (serves 2–4)

POWER LEVEL: 100% (FULL)

These rissoles are cooked in a browning dish

1 Place the onion in a large covered dish and cook for 3 min, stirring once throughout.
2 Add the rice, breadcrumbs, almonds, nutmeg, salt and pepper and beaten egg. Mix well together and form into 4 cakes or rissoles.
3 Preheat a browning dish for 5 min and brush the dish with a little oil. Cook the rissoles for 2½ min on the first side, turn them over and cook for a further 1½–2 min on the second side.
4 Serve hot or cold with a mixed salad.

1 onion, chopped
75g (3oz) cooked long-grain
    brown rice (page 77)
100g (4oz) wholewheat
    breadcrumbs
100g (4oz) ground almonds
½ × 5ml tsp (½tsp) grated
    nutmeg
salt and pepper
1 egg, beaten
oil
for serving: mixed salad

Vegetables and Salads

The daily supply of fresh vegetables and salads available throughout the year provides the wholefood microwave kitchen with a treasure chest of ingredients. Almost any variety from the most usual to the more exotic can be used in countless different ways, whether added raw to salads or cooked to form composite dishes for serving as starters, main courses, lunch or supper dishes.

Microwave-cooked vegetables look and taste better than those cooked by any other method and, because they are cooked so quickly in their own juices with very little extra liquid or butter, retain their natural flavours, crisp textures and full colours. Most important, too, for the wholefood cook is that the nutrient loss from vegetables cooked this way is negligible, thus saving valuable trace-element vitamin C and fragile B vitamins.

Cooking vegetables

Covered casserole dishes or mixing bowls which are suitable for use in the microwave may be used to cook the vegetables. Boiling bags and roasting bags are also ideal as the bag may easily be shaken or turned over to stir the contents during the cooking process. Remember though that the wire ties supplied with some makes must not be used—loosely tied string or rubber bands or simply twisting the neck of the bag are suitable alternatives.

Vegetables carry on cooking during their standing time out of the microwave and will remain hot for a considerable time. It is therefore possible to cook several varieties of vegetables one after another and serve them together. Reheating too is most successful as there is no drying out or loss in quality, which means that vegetables may be cooked in advance to be quickly reheated later after the main dish has been prepared.

Points to remember

* Prepare and cut vegetables into evenly sized pieces where possible.
* Do not overseason vegetables, as this can have a toughening effect. Adjust the seasoning at the end of cooking.
* A few drops of lemon juice sprinkled over peeled potatoes will prevent them from blackening during cooking.
* Vegetables cooked in their skins, ie jacket potatoes and whole tomatoes, should be scored or pricked well to prevent them bursting during cooking.
* The times given in the cooking chart (page 88) are intended as a guide, as the age and thickness of the vegetables will affect the cooking time. Take care not to overcook as the vegetables will continue to cook for a short while during their standing time.
* If the quantity of food to be cooked is increased, the time should be adjusted accordingly. For example, one jacket potato weighing 100–150g (4–5oz) will take 5–6 min, two will take 7–9 min and three will take 10–11 min, and so on.

Drying herbs

Many varieties of herbs are annual plants and, when near the end of their season, can be dried by microwave to last through the winter months. Compared with conventional methods, preserving herbs by drying in the microwave is extremely fast, and small quantities can be processed successfully, retaining better colours and aromas than conventionally dried herbs.

Indian Yoghurt Drink (page 40);
Spiced Aubergine Dip (page 41);
Curried Vegetable Rice (page 80);
Do-piaza (page 60)

Preferably the herbs should be clean and dry when picked, otherwise wash them thoroughly and pat dry between pieces of kitchen paper towel. Gently squeeze out as much moisture as possible after washing, as this will give better results. Remove the leaves from the stems (where applicable) and measure about 1 cupful of the leaves. Spread these out evenly on two thicknesses of kitchen paper towel to help absorb moisture during the heating process, cover with two more pieces of towel. Heat on 100% (full) setting for 4–6 min, turning over the paper towel (with the herbs) once throughout. Check after the minimum time—when dry, the herbs will be brittle and break very easily. Leave to cool between the paper before crushing and storing in an airtight jar which should be kept in a cool, dry place.

Vegetable cooking chart

Vegetable and quantity	Preparation	Amount of salted water to be added	Cooking time in min 100% (full)
artichokes, jerusalem 450g (1lb)	peel and cut into even size pieces	4 × 15ml tbsp (4tbsp) or 25g (1oz) butter	8–10
asparagus 225g (8oz)	trim and leave whole	2 × 15ml tbsp (2tbsp)	thin spears 6–8 thick spears 8–10
aubergines 450g (1lb)	wash, slice, sprinkle with salt and leave for 30 min, rinse	2 × 15ml tbsp (2tbsp)	8–10
beans, broad 450g (1lb)	remove from pods	3 × 15ml tbsp (3tbsp)	8–10
beans, french 450g (1lb)	wash and cut	2 × 15ml tbsp (2tbsp)	8–10
beans, runner 450g (1lb)	string and slice	2 × 15ml tbsp (2tbsp)	8–10
beetroot 450g (1lb)	peel and slice	2 × 15ml tbsp (2tbsp)	7–8
225g (8oz) whole	prick skin, wrap in clingfilm		12–15
broccoli 450g (1lb)	trim, cut into spears	2 × 15ml tbsp (2tbsp)	8–12
brussels sprouts 450g (1lb)	wash, remove outer leaves and trim	2 × 15ml tbsp (2tbsp)	8–10
cabbage 450g (1lb)	wash and shred finely	2 × 15ml tbsp (2tbsp)	8–10
carrots 225g (8oz)	*new* wash, scrape and cut into strips or leave whole, depending on size	2 × 15ml tbsp (2tbsp)	7–10
	old scrape or peel and slice	2 × 15ml tbsp (2tbsp)	7–10
cauliflower 675g (1½lb)	wash and cut into florets	4 × 15ml tbsp (4tbsp)	10–11
450g (1lb) whole	trim outside leaves, wash	4 × 15ml tbsp (4tbsp)	10–11
celery 350g (12oz)	wash, trim and slice	3 × 15ml tbsp (3tbsp)	10–12

corn on the cob 2 × 225g (8oz)	wash and trim	4 × 15ml tbsp (4tbsp) or 40g (1½oz) butter	6–8
courgettes 450g (1lb)	wash, trim and slice	—	8–10
curly kale 225g (8oz)	remove thicker stalks, wash thoroughly	4 × 15ml tbsp (4tbsp)	10–12
leeks 450g (1lb)	wash, trim and slice	2 × 15ml tbsp (2tbsp)	7–10
marrow 450g (1lb)	peel, cut into 2cm (¾in) rings, remove seeds and quarter the rings	2 × 15ml tbsp (2tbsp)	8–10
mushrooms 225g (8oz)	peel or wipe or wash	2 × 15ml tbsp (2tbsp) of stock or 25g (1oz) butter	5–6
okra 450g (1lb)	wash, trim, sprinkle with salt, leave for 30 min, rinse	2 × 15ml tbsp (2tbsp) or 25g (1oz) butter or oil	8–10
onions 225g (8oz)	peel and slice	2 × 15ml tbsp (2tbsp) or 25g (1oz) butter or oil	5–7
parsnips 450g (1lb)	peel and slice	2 × 15ml tbsp (2tbsp)	8–10
peas 225g (8oz)	remove from pods	2 × 15ml tbsp (2tbsp)	8–10
potatoes 450g (1lb)	peel and cut into even size pieces	4 × 15ml tbsp (4tbsp) or 25g (1oz) butter	8–10
potatoes, new, in their jackets 450g (1lb)	wash thoroughly	2 × 15ml tbsp (2tbsp)	10–12
potatoes, old, in their jackets 450g (1lb)	wash and scrub thoroughly, dry and prick skins	—	10–12
spinach 450g (1lb)	break up thicker stalks, wash thoroughly	—	6–8
spring greens 450g (1lb)	break up thicker stalks, wash and shred	2 × 15ml tbsp (2tbsp)	8–10
swedes 450g (1lb)	peel and dice	2 × 15ml tbsp (2tbsp)	6–7
tomatoes 450g (1lb)	wash and halve, place in shallow dish and cover with lid or clingfilm	—	6–8
turnips 450g (1lb)	peel and dice	2 × 15ml tbsp (2tbsp)	8–10

225g (8oz) chick peas
boiling water
1 × 200g (7oz) can tuna in
brine, drained
1 small onion
1 × 15ml tbsp (1tbsp) chopped
parsley
1 lemon, grated rind
2 × 15ml tbsp (2tbsp) lemon
juice
6 × 15ml tbsp (6tbsp) olive or
sunflower oil
pinch dry mustard
salt and pepper
for garnish: chopped parsley

Chick pea and tuna salad (*serves 4*)   *colour opposite*
POWER LEVEL: 100% (FULL) AND 50%

1 Place the chick peas in a large bowl and cover with boiling water. Cover the bowl and cook for 5 min, then allow to stand for 1 hr.
2 Rinse and drain the chick peas and cover with fresh boiling water. Cover the bowl with a lid or pierced clingfilm and cook for 10 min on 100% (full) setting and a further 25–30 min on 50%, or until soft. Drain and allow to cool.
3 Flake the tuna and mix with the chopped onion. Add the chick peas and chopped parsley. Season well and stir in the grated lemon rind.
4 Place the lemon juice, oil and mustard for the dressing in a small screw-top jar with some salt and pepper. Put the lid on, and shake well. Alternatively, whisk the ingredients together in a small bowl.
5 Transfer the fish and chick peas to a serving dish. Add the dressing, and toss well. Chill for at least an hour before serving and toss again, adding chopped parsley for garnish.

Note: *Fresh tuna is available in some fishmongers and may be cooked and used in place of the canned fish if preferred*

450g (1lb) new potatoes,
scrubbed
pinch salt
2 × 15ml tbsp (2tbsp) water
1 small sprig of mint
2 large oranges
150ml (¼pt) natural yoghurt
1 × 15ml tbsp (1tbsp) freshly
chopped mint
salt and pepper

Minted new potato and orange salad (*serves 3–4*)
POWER LEVEL: 100% (FULL)   *colour opposite*

1 Place the potatoes in a bowl, add the salt, water and sprig of mint, then cover and cook for 10–12 min, stirring once or twice throughout. Drain and allow to cool.
2 Remove all the rind and pith from the oranges and cut into segments, reserving any juice.
3 When the potatoes are cold, cut into thick slices and place in a serving dish. Add the orange segments and juice. Mix the yoghurt with the chopped mint, season, and pour over the salad. Toss lightly and chill well before serving.

DO NOT FREEZE

175g (6oz) wholewheat pasta,
cooked (page 69 and
method 1)
½ red pepper, diced
½ green pepper, diced
1 courgette, trimmed and diced
2 small carrots, peeled and
diced
75g (3oz) mushrooms, trimmed
and sliced
40g (1½oz) almonds or
walnuts, chopped
50g (2oz) raisins
salt and pepper
2 eggs
1 × 15ml tbsp (1tbsp) vinegar
½ × 5ml tsp (½tsp) mustard
275ml (½pt) sunflower oil,
approximately
for garnish: chopped parsley

Pasta salad (*serves 4*)   *colour page 23*
POWER LEVEL: 100% (FULL)

1 Cook the pasta, drain, rinse under cold running water and reserve. Prepare the vegetables.
2 Mix together the pasta and the vegetables in a serving dish, add the nuts and raisins and season with salt and pepper.
3 For the mayonnaise, place the eggs in a blender or food processor with the vinegar, mustard and salt and pepper. Blend for 1 min, then gradually add the oil whilst the machine is running until the mayonnaise is thick. Correct the seasoning.
4 Pour the mayonnaise over the salad and toss well. Chill before serving, garnished with chopped parsley.

DO NOT FREEZE

Chick Pea and Tuna Salad (above); Minted New Potato and Orange Salad (above); Soya Bean and Beansprout Salad (page 92)

225g (8oz) soya beans
boiling water
175g (6oz) beanshoots
1 medium onion, sliced
1 red pepper, deseeded and cut
　into strips
salt and ground black pepper
4 × 15ml tbsp (4tbsp)
　sunflower oil
2 × 15ml tbsp vinegar
1 clove garlic, crushed
1 × 5ml tsp (1tsp) chopped
　rosemary

Soya bean and beansprout salad (serves 4–6)   colour page 91
POWER LEVEL: 100% (FULL) AND 50%

1　Place the soya beans in a large bowl, cover with boiling water, cover the bowl with a lid and heat for 5 min. Allow to stand for 1 hr.
2　Rinse and drain the beans. Cover with fresh boiling water and cover the dish. Cook for 10 min on 100% (full) setting and a further 20–25 min on 50%, until tender. Drain and allow to cool.
3　Combine the soya beans with the beanshoots, onion and pepper. Season well with salt and pepper.
4　For the dressing, place the oil and vinegar in a small screw-top jar with the garlic and rosemary and a little black pepper. Screw on the lid and shake well to blend. Alternatively, whisk the ingredients together in a small bowl.
5　Pour the dressing over the salad and toss well. Chill the salad and toss again before serving.

DO NOT FREEZE

6 large, firm bananas
1 apple, peeled, cored and
　grated
2 × 15ml tbsp (2tbsp) lemon
　juice
25g (1oz) sunflower margarine
1 large onion, peeled and finely
　sliced
1 clove garlic, finely chopped
1–2 × 5ml tsp (1–2tsp) curry
　powder
1 × 5ml tsp (1tsp) turmeric
2 sticks celery, thickly sliced
150ml (¼pt) mayonnaise
　(page 22)
150ml (¼pt) natural yoghurt
salt to taste
for serving: plainly boiled rice
　(page 77) and desiccated
　coconut

Banana salad (serves 6–8)   colour page 7
POWER LEVEL: 100% (FULL)

This unusual salad is flavoured with curry powder and may be served as a main course or as part of a buffet menu

1　Peel and slice the bananas, mix with the grated apple. Sprinkle with the lemon juice.
2　Melt the margarine for 1 min in a large bowl, add the onion and garlic. Cover and cook for 2–3 min.
3　Add the curry powder and turmeric, stir well, cover and cook for 2 min.
4　Stir in the bananas, apple and celery, cover and cook for 4 min to heat through and combine the flavours. Leave to cool.
5　Mix the mayonnaise with the yoghurt, stir into the cold banana mixture and add salt to taste.
6　Pile into the centre of a bed of cooked, cold rice and serve chilled, sprinkled with desiccated coconut.

Note: Chopped, cooked chicken may be added to the dish, in which case a little more mayonnaise or yoghurt will be needed to blend the mixture

DO NOT FREEZE

1 head of celery
1 × 15ml tbsp (1tbsp) freshly
　chopped mixed herbs,
　eg chives, rosemary, basil
1 lemon, grated rind and juice
salt and pepper
1 × 15ml tbsp (1tbsp) dark
　demerara sugar
for garnish: 1–2 × 5ml tsp
　(1–2tsp) freshly chopped
　mixed herbs

Celery with herbs and lemon (serves 3–4)   colour page 11
POWER LEVEL: 100% (FULL)

1　Divide the celery into sticks, trim and wash. Cut into 12mm (½in) slices and place in a large dish.
2　Add the herbs and lemon rind and juice. Mix well, cover and cook, allowing approximately 15 min per 450g (1lb). Stir once or twice during cooking.
3　Season well and salt and pepper and add the sugar.
4　Serve hot as a vegetable or cold dressed with soured cream as a salad, garnished with freshly chopped mixed herbs.

Ratatouille *(serves 4–6)*   *colour page 7*
POWER LEVEL: 100% (FULL)

1   Sprinkle the prepared aubergines and courgettes with salt. Allow to stand for 30 min, then wash thoroughly.
2   Heat the oil in a large casserole for 3–4 min, add the onion and garlic and cook for 3 min.
3   Add the aubergines and courgettes and cook for 3 min. Add the peppers, tomatoes and seasoning to taste.
4   Cover and cook for 20–22 min, stirring 2–3 times throughout.
5   Serve hot or cold.

2 medium aubergines, sliced
225g (8oz) courgettes, sliced
salt
2 × 15ml tbsp (2tbsp) oil
1 large onion, sliced
2 cloves garlic, finely chopped
1 red pepper, deseeded and
   finely sliced
1 green pepper, deseeded and
   finely sliced
225g (8oz) tomatoes, skinned
   and roughly chopped
freshly ground black pepper

Aubergine flan *(serves 4)*
POWER LEVEL: 100% (FULL)

1   Place the sliced aubergine in a colander, sprinkling each layer generously with salt. Leave to stand for 1 hr.
2   Place the flour in a bowl with the salt, and rub in the butter or margarine until it resembles fine breadcrumbs. Mix to a manageable dough with tepid water. Knead on a lightly floured surface and roll out to fit a 20cm (8in) flan ring.
3   Place small pieces of foil around the upright edges of the pastry flan case and prick the base with a fork. Line the flan case with kitchen paper towel and fill with baking beans. Cook for 4 min, uncovered, then remove the baking beans, kitchen paper and foil and continue to cook for a further 2 min.
4   Place the onion and garlic in a large dish, cover and cook for 4 min, stirring once throughout. Add the tomato, lemon rind and juice, seasoning and herbs. Thoroughly rinse the aubergine, drain well and add to the dish. Cover and cook for 10–12 min, stirring once.
5   Stir the cheese and olives into the mixture and correct the seasoning. Pour the vegetables into the cooked flan case and smooth the top. Serve hot or cold.

1 large aubergine, trimmed
   and finely sliced
salt
175g (6oz) wholewheat flour
pinch salt
75g (3oz) butter or vegetable
   margarine
tepid water to mix
1 large onion, chopped
2 cloves garlic, crushed
1 large tomato, skinned and
   sliced
1 lemon, grated rind and juice
salt and pepper
1 × 5ml tsp (1tsp) dried
   oregano or basil
75g (3oz) fetta cheese, cubed
10 black olives

100g (4oz) bacon, de-rinded
  and diced
50g (2oz) desiccated coconut
1 small onion, chopped
675g (1½lb) spinach, washed
  and stalks removed
salt and pepper

Spinach with bacon and coconut (*serves 4*)   *colour opposite*
POWER LEVEL: 100% (FULL)

1 Place the bacon, coconut and onion in a large dish. Cover and cook for 4 min, stirring once halfway through.
2 Shake off any excess water from the spinach leaves. Stir into the dish, cover and cook for 8–10 min, stirring once or twice and using a spoon to break up the leaves.
3 Drain off any excess liquid, season well with salt and plenty of black pepper, and serve immediately.

550–675g (1¼–1½lb) carrots
150ml (¼pt) salted water
75g (3oz) curd or farmhouse
  cheddar cheese, grated
ground black pepper
½ × 5ml tsp (½tsp) ground
  nutmeg
½ × 5ml tsp (½tsp) dark
  demerara sugar, optional
for garnish: 1 × 15ml tbsp
  (1tbsp) chopped parsley

Carrot purée with cheese (*serves 4–6*)   *colour opposite*
POWER LEVEL: 100% (FULL)

1 Peel the carrots and slice very thinly. Place in a casserole dish with the salted water and cover. Cook for 12–15 min until tender, shaking or stirring twice throughout. Allow to stand for a few minutes.
2 Turn the carrots and liquid into a food processor or blender and purée. Add the curd or grated cheddar cheese, pepper, nutmeg and sugar, and purée again, scraping down the sides of the bowl if necessary.
3 Turn the purée back into the casserole dish and reheat for 1–1½ min until bubbling. Sprinkle with chopped parsley before serving.

for the pancakes:
1 egg
pinch salt
275ml (½pt) milk
100g (4oz) wholewheat flour
oil for frying

for the filling:
450g (1lb) cauliflower, cut into
  tiny florets
1 large onion, chopped
2–3 × 15ml tbsp (2–3tbsp)
  water
25g (1oz) sunflower margarine
25g (1oz) wholewheat flour
275ml (½pt) milk
50g (2oz) gruyère or farmhouse
  cheddar cheese, grated
1 × 15ml tbsp (1tbsp) freshly
  chopped tarragon or 1 × 5ml
  tsp (1tsp) dried tarragon
salt and pepper
150ml (¼pt) natural yoghurt
for garnish: sprigs tarragon

Cauliflower and tarragon pancakes (*serves 3–4*)   *colour opposite*
POWER LEVEL: 100% (FULL) AND 70%

The pancakes are cooked conventionally, the filling is prepared and cooked in the microwave

1 Prepare the pancake batter by blending the egg, salt and milk in a blender or food processor and then adding the flour, or whisk all the ingredients together in a bowl.
2 Cook 6–8 large pancakes from the batter in a frying pan on a hotplate, using a little oil to prevent them from sticking. Stack the pancakes until required, separating them with pieces of kitchen paper towel.
3 Make sure that the cauliflower is in very tiny florets. Using 100% (full) setting, cook the onion in a covered dish for 2 min. Stir well and add the cauliflower with the water. Cover and cook for 6–8 min until the cauliflower is soft, stirring once during cooking.
4 Melt the margarine for 1 min, add the flour and stir well. Gradually add the milk and any liquid from the cauliflower. Heat for 4–5 min until boiling and thickened, stirring every minute.
5 Add the grated cheese and tarragon to the sauce and season to taste.
6 Combine the sauce with the cauliflower and use a little of the mixture to fill each pancake. Roll the pancakes up and place on a serving dish.
7 Cover the dish and heat for 6 min on 70% setting. Remove the cover and pour the yoghurt over the pancakes. Heat for a further 1½–2 min on 100% (full).
8 Garnish with sprigs of tarragon before serving.

Spinach with Bacon and Coconut (above); Cauliflower and Tarragon Pancakes (above); Carrot Purée with Cheese (above)

2 × 15ml tbsp (2tbsp)
   sunflower oil
675g (1½lb) red cabbage,
   finely shredded
3 cloves garlic, crushed
1 bulb fennel, weighing
   approximately 225g (8oz),
   trimmed and sliced
225g (8oz) onions, sliced
salt and pepper
1 bay leaf
150ml (¼pt) red wine
1 × 5ml tsp (1tsp) caraway
   seeds

Red cabbage with fennel (*serves 4–6*)   *colour page 11*
POWER LEVEL: 100% (FULL)

1 Heat the oil in a large dish for 2 min. Add the cabbage, toss in the oil, then cover and cook for 6 min, stirring once.
2 Add remaining ingredients except the caraway seeds and mix well.
3 Cover the dish with a lid or pierced clingfilm. Cook for 10 min, stir and cook for a further 5–10 min. Correct the seasoning, and sprinkle with the caraway seeds before serving.

2 small savoy or similar
   cabbages
25g (1oz) sunflower margarine
1 medium leek, washed,
   trimmed and thinly sliced
50g (2oz) mushrooms, sliced
75g (3oz) curd cheese
salt
½ × 5ml tsp (½tsp) paprika
150ml (¼pt) boiling water
25g (1oz) sunflower margarine
100g (4oz) mushrooms, diced
25g (1oz) wholewheat flour
milk

Stuffed cabbages with mushroom sauce (*serves 4*)
POWER LEVEL: 100% (FULL) AND 60%

1 Remove the outer leaves of the cabbages, leaving a tightly balled heart. Wash thoroughly under running water and cut vertically into halves, towards the stalk of each cabbage.
2 Carefully remove the centre of each cabbage, leaving a shell approximately 12mm (½in) wide. Slit the stalks. Place the cabbage shells in a large shallow dish, cover and cook for 5 min. Shred the centres.
3 Melt 25g (1oz) margarine in a large dish for 1 min. Add the shredded cabbage and the leek, cover and cook for 6 min, stirring once.
4 Add the sliced mushrooms to the cabbage and leek, and cook for 2 min. Beat in the curd cheese, and season the mixture with salt and paprika.
5 Spoon the filling into the cabbage shells. Pour the boiling water into the base of the dish. Cover, and cook for 15–20 min on 60% setting.
6 Melt 25g (1oz) margarine for 1 min. Add the diced mushrooms and cook for 2 min.
7 Place the cabbage halves on a serving plate. Measure the cooking liquid and make up to 275ml (½pt) with milk.
8 Stir the flour into the mushrooms. Gradually add the liquid, stirring well. Cook for 4–5 min until thickened, stirring every minute. Season the sauce with salt and paprika.
9 Pour the sauce over the cabbage halves, and sprinkle with paprika. Heat through for 3–4 min, and serve immediately.

Parsnips with honey and dill *(serves 3–4)* *colour page 67*
POWER LEVEL: 100% (FULL)

1 Place all the ingredients except the salt and pepper in a bowl or dish. Cover and cook for 8–10 min until tender, stirring once during cooking.
2 Season to taste with the salt and pepper. Sprinkle with a little extra dill before serving.

450g (1lb) parsnips, peeled and cut into matchsticks
1 orange, juice
2 × 5ml tsp (2tsp) freshly chopped dill or ½ × 5ml tsp (½tsp) dried dill
1 × 15ml tbsp (1tbsp) honey
salt and pepper
for garnish: fresh chopped or dried dill for sprinkling

Celeriac and mushroom salad *(serves 4)* *colour page 107*
POWER LEVEL: 100% (FULL)

1 Cook the celeriac in a covered dish with the salt and water for 8–10 min or until tender, stirring once during cooking. Drain well, toss the celeriac in the lemon juice and allow to cool.
2 Place the almonds on an ovenproof plate or dish and cook, uncovered, for 2–3 min or until browned, stirring occasionally. Leave to cool.
3 Beat the cheese, then beat the yoghurt into it. Add a pinch of grated nutmeg, the parsley and plenty of black pepper. Season to taste with salt.
4 Combine the celeriac, mushrooms and the cheese and yoghurt dressing. Transfer to a serving dish, and garnish with the browned almonds. Chill well before serving.

DO NOT FREEZE

450g (1lb) celeriac, scrubbed, trimmed and peeled
pinch salt
3 × 15ml tbsp (3tbsp) water
½ lemon, juice
25g (1oz) almonds, blanched
50g (2oz) curd cheese
150ml (¼pt) natural yoghurt
pinch grated nutmeg
1 × 15ml tbsp (1tbsp) chopped parsley
salt and ground black pepper
175g (6oz) mushrooms, trimmed and sliced

Tomato and mushroom crumble *(serves 4–6)*
POWER LEVEL: 100% (FULL)

1 Lightly grease a large round ovenware dish.
2 Mix the tomato sauce with the sliced mushrooms and place in the greased dish.
3 Sift the flour with the salt and mustard and rub in the butter or margarine finely. Stir in the grated cheese.
4 Sprinkle the crumble topping lightly over the tomato mixture and smooth the top.
5 Cook for 8–10 min, giving a quarter turn every 2 min if necessary until hot through and the crumble cooked.
6 Serve hot, garnished with tomato slices.

550ml (1pt) tomato sauce (page 25)
225g (8oz) mushrooms, washed and sliced
150g (6oz) wholewheat flour
½ × 5ml tsp (½tsp) salt
½ × 5ml tsp (½tsp) dry mustard
75g (3oz) butter or vegetable margarine
75g (3oz) cheese, finely grated
for garnish: tomato slices

Red tomato chutney *(makes about 1.1kg/2½lb)*
POWER LEVEL: 100% (FULL)

1 Place the onions in a large bowl, cover and cook for 5 min, stirring once.
2 Add the tomatoes and cook for a further 8 min, uncovered, until the vegetables are soft and pulpy. Stir once during cooking.
3 Add the salt, spices and vinegar. Cook for 5 min, stir; continue to cook for a further 5 min.
4 Add the sugar and stir well. Cook, uncovered, for 35–40 min until thick, stirring occasionally.
5 Pour into warmed jars, seal and label.

225g (8oz) onions, finely chopped
1.5kg (3lb) ripe tomatoes, skinned and chopped
15g (½oz) salt
1 × 5ml tsp (1tsp) paprika
good pinch of cayenne
150ml (¼pt) distilled malt vinegar
175g (6oz) dark demerara sugar

Fruits and Puddings

Do not think that, by eating wholefoods, desserts are forbidden from the menu. In fact, with the good selection of fresh fruits available, the range of sweet dishes which can be quickly prepared or cooked by microwave is almost never ending, and the advantage of this fast cooking method is that all the fresh flavours, vitamins and colours are retained with very little loss of the natural fruit juices. If you prefer something sweet—and who doesn't sometimes—by using raw cane sugar or honey instead of refined white sugar, you can make really mouthwatering desserts.

Fruit purées are delicious, either served on their own or mixed into natural yoghurt or soured cream. They can also provide a base for something more special such as a mousse or soufflé. In the winter months, when the variety of fresh fruits available is limited, a selection of dried fruits will ring the changes at mealtimes. They can be served on their own or added to fresh fruit salads and, because of their natural sweetness, you will be able to cut down on the amount of other sweetener you use. In addition, dried fruits can be quickly soaked and cooked in the microwave for a hot fruit compôte, or to make a purée.

Flans made with wholewheat flour and toppings for crumbles made from oats, wholewheat flour and demerara sugar are most successful cooked in the microwave. (Traditional pies with pastry lids are not so good as the filling tends to boil out before the pastry is cooked.) Those steamed puddings of yesteryear which took hours to cook over a steamer are now cooked in just a fraction of the time in the microwave, and wholewheat flour can be substituted for white flour in most microwave pudding recipes.

Natural yoghurt is a good accompaniment for most desserts and puddings—providing a tangy contrast to anything sweet—although a hot alternative would be a custard made with fresh eggs and milk.

Also included in this section are a few recipes for wholefood fruit preserves. Refer to these as a guide when using other fruit preserve recipes.

Cooking dried fruits

For best results, dried fruits should be soaked before cooking. Although they can be cooked without this, the resulting fruits will not be so tender or plump. The fruits can either be soaked for 6–8 hr or overnight, or heated in a covered dish, with water, in the microwave for 6–10 min on 100% (full) setting, then allowed to stand for about 1 hr to plump and soften. After soaking 225g (8oz) dried fruits, drain them and place in a suitable container. Add fruit juice, water, or water and wine mixed, some lemon rind or juice and demerara sugar or honey to taste. Cover and cook on 100% (full) setting for about 10 min, stirring halfway through. Leave to stand for a few minutes before serving.

Cooking fresh fruits

Prepare the fruit in the usual way and add a little honey to taste. Cook in a roasting or boiling bag in a similar way to fresh vegetables although when it is important that the fruit pieces do not break, cook them in a covered dish with the liquid quantity slightly increased. The fruit should be checked and

Blackcurrant Sorbet (page 101); Rødgrød (page 101); Banana Baked Pears (page 100)

stirred or turned regularly to make sure it does not overcook. Fruits cooked in their skins, such as baked apples, should first be pricked or scored to prevent bursting during the cooking process. As most fruits may be cooked without additional liquid, they can be sieved or puréed to make delicious sauces to pour over puddings, ice cream or natural yoghurt (page 36).

Fruit cooking chart

Fruit	Preparation	Cooking time	
		100% (full)	50%
cooking apples 450g (1lb)	peel, core and slice. Sprinkle with sugar or add honey to taste	6–8 min	11–15 min
apricots 450g (1lb)	halve and stone, add honey to taste and a few drops of lemon juice	6–8 min	11–15 min
peaches 4 medium size	halve and stone	4–5 min	7–8 min
pears 6 medium size	peel, halve and core. Add a pinch of cinnamon to a little hot water and sweeten to taste	8–10 min	15–20 min
plums, cherries, greengages, damsons 450g (1lb)	stone, add honey or sugar to taste and grated rind of a lemon	4–5 min	7–8 min
rhubarb 450g (1lb)	trim and cut into short lengths. Add 100–150g (4–5oz) demerara sugar and grated or pared rind of a lemon	7–10 min	14–20 min
soft fruits 450g (1lb)	top and tail currants, hull the berries. Wash well and add sweetener to taste	3–5 min	6–10 min

4 firm dessert pears, evenly sized and preferably with their stalks
1 lemon, grated rind and juice
1 small ripe banana
40g (1½oz) walnuts, finely chopped
1 × 5ml tsp (1tsp) light muscovado sugar
good pinch ground ginger
4 × 15ml tbsp (4tbsp) clear honey
for serving: natural yoghurt

Banana baked pears *(serves 4)*   *colour page 99*
POWER LEVEL: 60%

1 Cut a slice from the base of each pear so that it will stand on a plate. Carefully remove the core from the base, leaving a hollow for the stuffing.
2 Peel each pear and brush the fruit with lemon juice to prevent browning. Mash the banana with a fork and add the remaining lemon juice.
3 Reserve a few of the chopped walnuts and add the remainder to the banana. Stir in the sugar and ginger.
4 Carefully fill the base of each pear with the mixture then stand the pears on a serving plate. Spoon the honey over.
5 Cook, uncovered, for 8 min or until tender. Sprinkle with the remaining nuts mixed with the lemon rind. Serve immediately, handing the natural yoghurt separately.

DO NOT FREEZE

Blackcurrant sorbet *(serves 4–6)*   *colour page 99*
POWER LEVEL: 100% (FULL)

275ml (½pt) boiling water
100g (4oz) dark demerara sugar
225g (8oz) blackcurrants,
  topped and tailed
1 lemon, juice
water
2 egg whites

1   Place the boiling water and sugar in a bowl and stir well to dissolve the sugar. Cook, uncovered, for 10 min, then allow to cool.
2   Wash the blackcurrants, place in a covered dish and cook for 3–4 min until soft, stirring once throughout.
3   Purée the blackcurrants in a blender or food processor and add to the sugar syrup with the lemon juice. Measure the liquid and make up to 550ml (1pt) with water.
4   Pour the blackcurrant mixture into a shallow freezer container and freeze until firm.
5   Whisk the egg whites until stiff. Remove the blackcurrant mixture from its container and beat with a whisk or a fork to break up the set. Carefully fold in the egg whites with a metal spoon until evenly distributed.
6   Return the sorbet to the freezer container and freeze until solid.

Rødgrød *(serves 4)*   *colour page 99*
POWER LEVEL: 100% (FULL)

900g (2lb) redcurrants, washed
  and strung
2 × 15ml tbsp (2tbsp) light
  muscovado sugar
900g (2lb) raspberries
3 × 15ml tbsp (3tbsp)
  arrowroot
clear honey to taste
25g (1oz) flaked almonds

1   Place the redcurrants in a bowl with the sugar, cover and cook for 8–10 min until soft. Purée in a blender or processor, or rub through a sieve. Purée the raspberries and rub through a sieve to remove the pips.
2   Combine the two purées. Mix the arrowroot with a little of the purée and heat the remainder in a covered bowl for 5–6 min or until boiling.
3   Stir the arrowroot into the hot purée and continue to cook for a further 10 min, stirring every 2 min.
4   Sweeten the purée to taste with the honey, and allow to cool slightly before pouring into individual serving dishes.
5   Place the flaked almonds on a heat-resistant plastic or glass plate and cook, uncovered, for 2–3 min until browned, stirring once.
6   Sprinkle a few of the almonds onto each rødgrød and chill before serving.

75g (3oz) sultanas
75g (3oz) raisins
100g (4oz) figs, roughly
  chopped
275ml (½pt) apple juice
100g (4oz) wholewheat
  breadcrumbs
100g (4oz) wholewheat flour
2 × 5ml tsp (2tsp) mixed spice
25g (1oz) brazil nuts, roughly
  chopped
25g (1oz) walnuts, roughly
  chopped
50g (2oz) almonds, roughly
  chopped
2 bananas, mashed
2 eggs, beaten
oil
for serving: natural yoghurt or
egg custard sauce (page 24)

Rich fruit and nut pudding *(serves 6–8)*   *colour opposite*
POWER LEVEL: 100% (FULL) AND 50%

This pudding is sweetened completely by the ingredients that are used. It is quite rich and would make an interesting wholefood alternative to Christmas pudding

1 Place the sultanas, raisins and figs in a bowl, add the apple juice, cover and heat for 5 min. Leave to stand for 10 min.
2 Add all the remaining ingredients to the bowl and mix well.
3 Turn the mixture into a lightly oiled 1.1 litre (2pt) pudding basin—the mixture will not fill the bowl completely. Cover the bowl with pierced clingfilm.
4 Cook on 50% setting for 15–18 min. Allow to stand for 5 min.
5 Turn out onto a serving plate. Serve hot with natural yoghurt or egg custard sauce.

825ml (1½pt) apple juice
100g (4oz) each dried apples,
  prunes and figs
175g (6oz) dried apricots
25g (1oz) walnuts, chopped

Apple fruit compôte *(serves 4)*   *colour opposite*
POWER LEVEL: 100% (FULL)

1 Place the apple juice in a large bowl, cover and heat for 4 min. Add the dried fruits, cover and cook for 6 min. Allow to stand for 45–60 min until plump.
2 Cover and cook for 10 min until the fruits are tender. Sprinkle with the chopped walnuts and serve hot or cold.

550g (1¼lb) cooking apples,
  peeled, cored and sliced
100g (4oz) dates, stoned and
  chopped
100g (4oz) medium oatmeal
50g (2oz) bran
75g (3oz) butter or vegetable
  margarine
50g (2oz) dark demerara sugar

Date and apple oat crumble *(serves 4–6)*   *colour opposite*
POWER LEVEL: 70%

1 Place the apples and dates in the bottom of a 1.4–1.7 litre (2½–3pt) dish and mix well together.
2 Prepare the crumble by placing the oatmeal and bran in a bowl and rubbing in the butter or vegetable margarine. Stir in the sugar, then spoon the crumble mixture over the apples.
3 Cook, uncovered, for 15–18 min until the topping is cooked. Leave for a few minutes before serving hot.

900g (2lb) loganberries
900g (2lb) dark demerara sugar

*Rich Fruit and Nut Pudding
(above); Apple Fruit Compôte
(above); Date and Apple Oat
Crumble (above)*

Loganberry jam *(makes about 2kg/4lb)*
POWER LEVEL: 100% (FULL)

1 Wash the loganberries and place them in a large bowl. Cover and cook for 8 min or until soft, stirring once throughout.
2 Add the sugar and stir well. Cook the jam in the microwave, uncovered, for 20–25 min or until setting point is reached.
3 Pour into warmed jars, seal and label.

50g (2oz) blanched hazelnuts
100g (4oz) sunflower margarine
100g (4oz) light muscovado
    sugar
2 eggs
100g (4oz) wholewheat flour
1 × 5ml tsp (1tsp) baking
    powder
3–4 × 15ml tbsp (3–4tbsp) milk
225g (8oz) raspberries
150ml (¼pt) water
4–5×15ml tbsp (4–5tbsp) clear
    honey
450g (1lb) red cherries, stoned
275ml (½pt) natural yoghurt
3 × 15ml tbsp (3tbsp) soured
    cream
3 egg yolks
2 × 5ml tsp (2tsp) arrowroot
225g (8oz) strawberries,
    chopped

Summer sunset trifle (serves 6–8)   colour page 23
POWER LEVEL: 100% (FULL) AND 60%

1   Lightly oil a 17.5cm (7in) microwave cake dish or similar container.
2   Place the hazelnuts on a heat-resistant plastic or glass plate and cook, uncovered, for 3–4 min on 100% (full) setting until browned, tossing them over once during cooking. Grind the nuts in a blender or food processor.
3   Place the margarine, sugar, eggs, 25g (1oz) of the ground hazelnuts, flour, baking powder and milk in a bowl or food processor and beat until well mixed. (The mixture may appear slightly curdled—this is because of the grain of the flour.)
4   Place the mixture in the prepared dish and cook for 5 min on 60% setting, then a further 1½–2 min on 100% (full). Allow to stand for 5 min before turning out onto a cooling rack.
5   Purée the raspberries and sieve to remove the pips. Add the water and 2–3 × 15ml tbsp (2–3tbsp) clear honey to taste. Heat for 2–3 min, and stir until blended.
6   Break the cooled hazelnut sponge cake into pieces and place in the base of a large glass bowl. Pour the raspberry purée over the sponge.
7   Cook the stoned cherries in a covered dish for 3–4 min on 100% (full) until the skins are just soft, stirring once throughout. Spoon the cherries over the raspberry purée in the bowl.
8   Beat together the yoghurt, soured cream, 2 × 15ml tbsp (2tbsp) clear honey, egg yolks and arrowroot in a bowl, and heat in the microwave for 4–5 min on 100% (full) until thickened, stirring every minute. Add the chopped strawberries, stir well and pour the custard over the trifle.
9   Decorate the trifle with the remaining hazelnuts and chill before serving.

DO NOT FREEZE

oil
225g (8oz) wholewheat flour
2 × 5ml tsp (2tsp) baking
    powder
pinch salt
75g (3oz) butter or vegetable
    margarine
75g (3oz) light muscovado
    sugar
1 egg, beaten
milk
150ml (¼pt) double cream,
    whipped
350–450g (¾–1lb) strawberries

Wholewheat strawberry shortcake (serves 6)
POWER LEVEL: 60%

1   Lightly oil a deep 17.5–20cm (7–8in) round dish and line the base with a circle of greased greaseproof paper or baking parchment.
2   Place the flour, baking powder and salt in a bowl and rub in the butter or margarine. Add the sugar and beaten egg and mix to a smooth light dough, adding a little milk if necessary.
3   Knead the dough lightly on a floured surface and roll out to the correct size to fit the dish. Press the shortcake into the dish.
4   Cook, uncovered, for 6–6½ min on 60% setting. Allow to stand for a few minutes, then turn out onto a cooling rack. Leave until cold.
5   Place a little of the whipped cream in a piping bag fitted with a star nozzle, and leave in the refrigerator.
6   When the cake is completely cold, split in half and place the bottom on a serving plate. Spread with the remaining whipped cream. Reserve 6 evenly sized strawberries for decoration and chop the rest. Pile the chopped strawberries onto the cream.
7   Cut the top of the cake into 6 wedges and arrange over the strawberries. Pipe each section with a rosette of cream and decorate with a whole strawberry.
8   Serve chilled.

DO NOT FREEZE

Baked stuffed peaches with raspberry sauce *(serves 4)*
POWER LEVEL: 100% (FULL) AND 60%

1 Heat each peach on 100% (full) setting for 45–60 sec, then remove the skins. Cut the peaches in half, remove the stones and place the fruit in a suitable serving dish.
2 Cover the dish with a lid or pierced clingfilm and cook the peaches on 60% setting for 5–6 min or until they are just tender.
3 Mix together 100g (4oz) raspberries, almonds, honey and soured cream to make the filling. Fill each peach half and pile the remaining mixture over the top of the peaches.
4 Make the sauce by cooking the 225g (8oz) raspberries in a covered dish for 3–4 min on 100% (full) until soft, stirring once during cooking. Sweeten the fruit to taste using either light muscovado sugar or honey, and rub the mixture through a sieve to remove the pips.
5 Heat the stuffed peaches, covered, for about 4–5 min on 60% setting until just hot. Serve warm or cold with the raspberry sauce—a little may be poured over the peaches and the rest handed separately.

Note: *Sauces made from soft fruits are very quick to prepare in the microwave. Wash and prepare the fruits and then cook in a covered dish, stirring once throughout and allowing 5–6 min per 450g (1lb) until soft. Sweeten the sauce to taste, then purée or sieve. Use with puddings and ice creams. See page 25*

4 firm peaches
50g (2oz) muesli
100g (4oz) raspberries, roughly chopped
25g (1oz) almonds, roughly chopped
1 × 15ml tbsp (1tbsp) honey
1 × 15ml tbsp (1tbsp) soured cream
225g (8oz) raspberries
light muscovado sugar or honey to taste

Rhubarb and orange brown betty *(serves 6)*
POWER LEVEL: 100% (FULL)

1 Cut the rhubarb into 3.75cm (1½in) lengths and place in a bowl with the orange rind, juice and cinnamon. Cook, covered, for 8–10 min until just soft, stirring once during cooking.
2 Remove the cinnamon stick and sweeten the rhubarb to taste with the honey.
3 Spread the slices of bread with the sunflower margarine. Cut 2 of the slices to fit a deep 17.5–20cm (7–8in) round dish.
4 Pour half the rhubarb over the bread and repeat with another layer of bread and rhubarb. Top the brown betty with the remaining bread cut into triangles.
5 Cook, uncovered, for 8 min or until the bread on top of the pudding is starting to crisp. Alternatively, cook in a hot conventional oven until golden brown.
6 Sprinkle the pudding with demerara sugar and serve immediately.

675g (1½lb) rhubarb, washed and trimmed
1 orange, grated rind and juice
5cm (2in) stick cinnamon
4 × 15ml tbsp (4tbsp) clear honey, approximately
6 large slices wholewheat bread, crusts removed
sunflower margarine
demerara sugar to taste

Hot raspberry snow *(serves 3–4)*
POWER LEVEL: 100% (FULL) AND 60%

1 Place the raspberries in a deep 15–17.5cm (6–7in) round dish with the sugar. Cover and cook for 3 min, and stir well.
2 Beat the yoghurt with the egg yolks, flour and almonds. Whisk the egg whites until stiff and fold in the yoghurt mixture.
3 Pile the topping onto the raspberries and cook on 60% setting for 5–6 min until set. Sprinkle with the sugar and serve immediately.

450g (1lb) raspberries
2–3 × 15ml tbsp (2–3tbsp) light muscovado sugar
150ml (¼pt) natural yoghurt
2 eggs, separated
15g (½oz) wholewheat flour
25g (1oz) ground almonds
1 × 15ml (1tbsp) light muscovado sugar for sprinkling

450g (1lb) dessert plums
1 × 5ml tsp (1tsp) ground
  cinnamon
3–4 × 15ml tbsp (3–4tbsp)
  clear honey
2 egg yolks
275ml (½pt) natural yoghurt
25–50g (1–2oz) light
  muscovado sugar
2 × 15ml tbsp (2tbsp) chopped
  walnuts

Plums with yoghurt *(serves 4)*
POWER LEVEL: 100% (FULL) AND 50%

1 Wash, halve and stone the plums. Place in a 17.5cm (7in) round dish with the cinnamon and honey. Cover and cook for 4 min, stirring once throughout.
2 Beat the egg yolks with the yoghurt and sugar to taste. Heat for 1½ min, whisking every 30 sec until heated through.
3 Pour the topping over the plums and cook at 50% for 5 min or until the topping is set.
4 Serve hot or cold, sprinkled with the chopped walnuts.

DO NOT FREEZE

75g (3oz) sunflower margarine
175g (6oz) muesli mix, finely
  ground
1 head elderflowers
450g (1lb) gooseberries, topped
  and tailed
275ml (½pt) water
3–4 × 15ml tbsp (3–4tbsp)
  clear honey
1 envelope plus 1 × 5ml tsp
  (1tsp) gelatin
225g (8oz) curd cheese
50g (2oz) light muscovado
  sugar
2 eggs, separated

Gooseberry and elderflower cheesecake *(serves 6–8)*
POWER LEVEL: 100% (FULL)   *colour opposite*

1 Melt the margarine in a bowl for 1 min. Add the muesli and mix well. Press the mixture into the bottom of a 20cm (8in) round loose-bottomed tin and chill in the refrigerator.
2 Tie the elderflowers in a piece of muslin or clean J-cloth. Place in a bowl with the gooseberries and water, cover and cook for 10 min, stirring once throughout. Discard the elderflowers and sweeten the gooseberries with honey to taste.
3 Drain 150ml (¼pt) of liquid from the gooseberries, sprinkle with the gelatin, stir well and leave to soften. Purée the gooseberries and remaining juice in a blender or food processor.
4 Cream the curd cheese with the sugar and egg yolks. Combine with the purée. If the gelatin has not dissolved completely, heat in the microwave for 30 sec, stir well, and then mix into the combined gooseberry purée. Chill until just beginning to set.
5 Whisk the egg whites until stiff, then fold into the gooseberry mixture. Pour onto the muesli base and leave to set.
6 Chill before removing from the tin and serving.

DO NOT FREEZE

*Gooseberry and Elderflower
Cheesecake (above); Celeriac and
Mushroom Salad (page 97);
Flageolets with Cod (page 76)*

175g (6oz) wholewheat flour
pinch salt
75g (3oz) butter or vegetable
  margarine
tepid water to mix
450g (1lb) blackcurrants,
  topped and tailed
50g (2oz) light muscovado
  sugar
25g (1oz) sunflower margarine
75g (3oz) ground almonds
3 eggs, separated
75g (3oz) light muscovado
  sugar

Blackcurrant and almond meringue pie *(serves 6)*
POWER LEVEL: 100% (FULL) AND 60%

1   Place the flour and salt in a bowl, add the butter or vegetable margarine and rub in until the mixture resembles breadcrumbs. Add sufficient tepid water to make a firm dough.
2   Roll out the pastry on a floured surface and use to line a 20cm (8in) flan ring. Place thin strips of aluminium foil around the upright edges of the pastry flan case and prick the base with a fork. Place pieces of kitchen paper towel in the base and fill the flan with baking beans.
3   Cook the flan case 'blind' for 4 min on 100% (full). Remove the beans, paper and foil and cook for a further 1½–2 min.
4   Wash the blackcurrants, and place in a dish with the sugar and sunflower margarine. Cover and cook for 6–8 min until soft, stirring once throughout. Allow to cool slightly before beating in the almonds and egg yolks. Pour the mixture into the flan case.
5   Whisk the egg whites until stiff. Break up the sugar with a fork and whisk into the egg whites. Pile the topping onto the flan.
6   Cook, uncovered, on 60% setting for 3–4 min until just set, or alternatively bake in a preheated conventional oven at 200°C (400°F) mark 6 until browned, about 10 min. Serve hot or cold.

DO NOT FREEZE

4 grapefruit
3 large lemons
825ml (1½pt) boiling water
1.8kg (4lb) demerara sugar

Grapefruit and lemon marmalade *(makes about 3½kg/7lb)*
POWER LEVEL: 100% (FULL)

Heating the whole fruits in the microwave allows the maximum amount of juice to be extracted. A softer peel will be achieved if the shreds are allowed to soak for approximately 1 hr before cooking

1   Wash and dry the fruits. Heat in the microwave for 2 min, then squeeze the juice from the fruits and place it in a large bowl.
2   Remove all the pith and pips, and tie in a muslin or a piece of clean J-cloth. Add the bag to the fruit juice.
3   Finely shred the peel and add to the bowl with the boiling water. Cover and cook for 25–30 min until the peel is tender. Stir once throughout.
4   Remove the muslin bag, add the sugar and stir well. Cook the marmalade for 20–25 min or until setting point is reached, stirring every 5 min.
5   Allow the marmalade to stand for 30–40 min before pouring into warmed jars, then seal and label.

450g (1lb) apricots, washed,
  halved and stoned
100g (4oz) sunflower margarine
2 lemons, grated rind and juice
2–3 × 15ml tbsp (2–3tbsp)
  demerara sugar, to taste
450g (1lb) wholewheat
  breadcrumbs or cake crumbs
1 × 5ml tsp (1tsp) mixed spice
1 × 15ml tbsp (1tbsp) demerara
  sugar for sprinkling
for serving: natural yoghurt

Apricot charlotte *(serves 6)*
POWER LEVEL: 100% (FULL)

1   Place the apricots in a bowl with 25g (1oz) of margarine, the lemon rind and juice and sugar to taste. Cover and cook for 6–8 min or until soft, stirring once throughout.
2   Melt the remaining margarine in a bowl for 2 min, add the crumbs and the mixed spice. Stir well to ensure that the crumbs are well coated.
3   Layer the crumbs and apricots in a 17.5–20cm (7–8in) round dish, starting and finishing with a layer of crumbs.
4   Cook, uncovered, for 5–6 min and sprinkle with the demerara sugar before serving. Serve hot or cold with natural yoghurt.

Baking

Among the delights of microwave baking are the near-instant results which can be achieved and the joy of watching a cake or yeast mixture rise up and cook as if by magic, knowing of the savings in time and energy over cooking by traditional methods. Baking by microwave dispels the idea that home baking has almost gone out of fashion in these days of convenience foods—and no commercially baked product can ever taste like a home-baked one.

The wholefood recipes given in this section are only a small number of the many that can be made. In fact, most microwave baking recipes can be adapted to use wholefoods by replacing white flour with wholewheat flour, refined sugars with demerara sugar or honey, and by using sunflower margarine instead of butter. Wholewheat flours absorb more moisture than white flours, so you may need to add a little more liquid. The 100% wholewheat strong flours are more suited to bread and rich cake mixtures, and you may prefer the finer 81% wholewheat flours for lighter cakes and sponges.

Cakes and biscuits

Home-made wholewheat cakes can be cooked in the microwave most successfully and have good, light textures. They do not obtain the traditional brown appearance as when baked conventionally, but many are 'self-coloured' anyway, and there is much to be said for them being cooked so quickly whether for the family or that unexpected guest. A wholefood microwave baked cake made with honey, unrefined sugar and wholewheat flour is full of flavour and very moist, so there is no need for icings or fondants for decoration. Instead, have available some clear honey for brushing over plain cakes before topping with chopped nuts. Sponges can be sandwiched together with the unrefined or low-sugar jams or sugarless fruit spreads available from health-food shops.

Any suitable container, including paper, may be used for cooking cakes, but straight-sided ones give good results and a better shape. The container may be lined with lightly greased greaseproof paper or with baking parchment, but do not sprinkle with flour as this will only result in a doughy crust being formed on the outside of the finished cake. Make sure that the container is sufficiently large to allow for the mixture to rise; as a general guide, only half fill the dish with mixture. Cakes with a high proportion of fruit require lower power settings for best results. The use of a microwave baking rack, or a cake dish with a rim on the base, will allow more efficient penetration of the microwave energy and help to prevent a moist base to the cake.

If, during the cooking process, the mixture should appear to rise unevenly, it will normally level out towards the end of the cooking period; if in doubt, just turn the container approximately every 2 min, although this may not be necessary if the cooker has a turntable. Overcooking causes dry, hard cakes, so remove from the oven when they seem slightly moist on top. As a general rule, when the cake has risen completely, give it 1 min more cooking time then remove from the microwave. Although it is not usually necessary, should the outside of the cake be set before the centre, it is possible to protect these outside edges by covering with smooth pieces of aluminium foil for the last few minutes of the cooking period. After cooking, allow the cake to stand for 10–15 min before removing it onto a cooling tray.

Not all biscuit recipes are successful in the microwave; better results are achieved with those mixtures which are cut into pieces after cooking. However, the few recipes included in this section are well worth trying.

Proving and cooking yeast doughs

Muesli Cake (below); Cottage Cheese
Tealoaf (below); Potato Girdle
Scones (page 112); Light German
Pumpernickel (page 112)

The advantage of proving dough in the microwave is that it is so fast—450g (1lb) bread dough can be proved in half the normal time required. The covered dough is given combinations of short bursts of microwave energy for 15 sec, with standing or resting periods of 5–15 min, allowing an even distribution of warmth through the dough ensuring a steady rise. You will find that, when proving the lighter yeast mixtures, 5–10 min standing times will be sufficient; but for the heavier doughs, 10–15 min periods will give better results.

After proving and shaping, the dough can be cooked by microwave in 6–7 min. This will produce a good-textured loaf with a soft crust. Of course it will not be browned as when baked conventionally; but if a crisper crust is preferred the dough can be partly cooked for 3–4 min in the microwave and then finished in a conventional oven, preheated to a high temperature, for 8–10 min. Alternatively, the dough can be prepared and proved by microwave and afterwards completely cooked conventionally. Loaves of bread and rolls which are to be proved and cooked in the microwave cooker must, of course, be placed in suitable microwave containers. The dough may be sprinkled with nibbed wheat, poppy seeds or sesame seeds for a more decorative finish.

Included in this section are some sweet yeast mixtures and a few breads which are leavened with soda rather than yeast.

175g (6oz) muesli
100g (4oz) molasses sugar
2 × 15ml tbsp (2tbsp) malt
    extract
175g (6oz) sultanas
225ml (8fl oz) apple juice,
    approximately
2 cooking apples, peeled and
    grated
175g (6oz) wholewheat flour
3 × 5ml tsp (3tsp) baking
    powder
1 × 5ml tsp (1tsp) mixed spice
for decoration: walnut halves

Muesli cake (*serves 8–12*)   *colour opposite*
POWER LEVEL: 100% (FULL) AND 50%

1   Lightly oil a deep 15–17.5cm (6–7in) round cake dish.
2   Place the muesli, molasses, malt extract, sultanas and apple juice in a bowl, cover and heat for 3 min on 100% (full) setting. Stir and allow to stand, covered, for 5 min.
3   Add the apple, flour, baking powder and spice to the muesli and mix well to a soft dropping consistency, adding a little more apple juice if necessary.
4   Turn the mixture into the prepared dish and cook, uncovered, for 20–25 min on 50% setting.
5   Allow to stand for a few minutes before turning out onto a cooling rack. Decorate with walnut halves.

225g (8oz) cottage cheese,
    sieved or puréed
175g (6oz) dark muscovado
    sugar
3 eggs, beaten
50g (2oz) walnuts, chopped
100g (4oz) pitted dates,
    chopped
225g (8oz) wholewheat flour
2 × 5ml tsp (2tsp) baking
    powder
pinch mixed spice
4 walnuts for decoration
butter or sunflower margarine
    for spreading

Cottage cheese tealoaf (*makes 1 loaf*)   *colour opposite*
POWER LEVEL: 100% (FULL) AND 60%

1   Lightly grease a large microwave loaf dish, measuring approximately 10 × 17.5 × 6cm (4 × 7 × 2½in).
2   Place the cottage cheese in a bowl, add the sugar and beat until creamy. Gradually beat the eggs into the mixture.
3   Add the walnuts and dates, then fold in the flour, baking powder and spice.
4   Turn the mixture into the prepared dish and press the 4 walnuts into the top. Cook for 6–7 min on 100% (full) setting and a further 2½–4 min on 60%. Stand for 5 min, then turn out onto a rack to cool.
5   Serve sliced, spread with butter or sunflower margarine.

175g (6oz) wholewheat flour
50g (2oz) rye flour
1 × 5ml tsp (1tsp) salt
15g (½oz) bran
15g (½oz) maize meal
65g (2½oz) cold mashed potato
40g (1½oz) sunflower
  margarine
150ml (¼pt) water
15g (½oz) fresh yeast
1 × 5ml tsp (1tsp) soft brown
  sugar

Light german pumpernickel *(makes 1 small loaf)*

POWER LEVEL: 100% (FULL)   *colour pages 7 and 11*

1 Place the flours and salt in a large bowl together with the bran, maize meal and cold mashed potato. Make a well in the centre.
2 Heat the margarine until melted, about 30 sec. Heat the water for 20 sec. Cream the yeast and sugar with a little of the liquid.
3 Add the margarine and yeast liquid to the dry ingredients with sufficient of the remaining liquid to give a workable dough.
4 Turn out onto a floured surface and knead until smooth. Clean the bowl and return the dough to it, covering with a lid or clingfilm. Heat for 15 sec, then allow to stand for 5–10 min. Repeat 4–5 times until doubled in size.
5 Knead again and shape to fit a small microwave loaf dish measuring 10 × 17.5 × 3.75cm (4 × 7 × 1½in). Loosely cover with clingfilm and prove again as above until the dough has risen to the top of the dish. Remove the clingfilm.
6 Cook for 3½–4 min, stand for 5 min, then turn onto a wire rack to cool. Serve thinly sliced and buttered, with cheese or cold meat.

450g (1lb) potatoes, cooked and
  mashed
1–2 × 5ml tsp (1–2tsp) salt
50g (2oz) butter or sunflower
  margarine
100g (4oz) wholewheat flour,
  approximately
oil

Potato girdle scones *(makes 12–16)*   *colour page 111*

POWER LEVEL: 100% (FULL)

1 Add salt to taste to the potatoes with the butter or margarine. Work in sufficient flour to give a stiff mixture.
2 Knead lightly on a floured surface and roll out to 6mm (¼in) thick. Cut into rounds with a 5cm (2in) cutter, or into triangles.
3 Preheat the browning dish for 4–5 min depending on size, and lightly brush the base with oil.
4 Quickly place half the scones in the browning dish, cook for 1 min, turn the scones over and the dish round, cook for 1½–2 min.
5 Reheat the browning dish for 1–2 min and cook the second batch as described previously.
6 Serve hot, spread with butter.

Note: *If using left-over cold potatoes, heat them through in the microwave after mashing, as hot potatoes give lighter scones*

Carrot cake (*serves 8*)
POWER LEVEL: 60% AND 100% (FULL)

1 Lightly oil a 17.5cm (7in) microwave ring mould.
2 Place the flour, spices and baking powder in a bowl and rub in the butter or margarine. Stir in the sugar, lemon rind, almonds and carrots.
3 Add the lemon juice and egg and beat well together. Place the mixture into the prepared dish and smooth the surface.
4 Cook, uncovered, for 5 min on 60% then for a further 1½ min on 100% (full) setting. Leave to stand for 5 min, then turn onto a rack to cool. Serve cut into slices.

100g (4oz) wholewheat flour
good pinch each cinnamon and nutmeg
1 × 5ml tsp (1tsp) baking powder
50g (2oz) butter or vegetable margarine
75g (3oz) dark demerara sugar
½ lemon, grated rind and juice
50g (2oz) ground almonds
100g (4oz) carrots, peeled and grated
1 egg, beaten
75ml (2½fl oz) milk

Basic wholewheat bread (*makes 1 loaf*)
POWER LEVEL: 100% (FULL)

1 Place the flour and salt in a bowl and rub in the margarine. Make a well in the centre.
2 Mix together the yeast and molasses. Heat the milk for 1 min and cream the yeast with a little of the liquid.
3 Pour the yeast liquid onto the flour with sufficient milk to make a workable dough. Turn onto a floured board and knead thoroughly until smooth.
4 Place in a bowl and cover with pierced clingfilm. Heat for 15 sec, allow to stand for 10–15 min. Repeat 5–6 times or until doubled in size (with a heavy wholewheat dough this process takes longer than for white bread).
5 Lightly oil a 17.5cm (7in) round deep dish. Knock the dough back lightly on a floured board and shape to fit the prepared dish. Place in the dough, cover with clingfilm, and heat for 15 sec. Allow to stand for 10–15 min. Repeat 3–4 times until well risen.
6 Remove the clingfilm, sprinkle a little flour on the dough and bake for 5–7 min. Allow to stand for 5 min, then turn the loaf out onto a rack to cool.

450g (1lb) wholewheat flour
1 × 5ml tsp (1tsp) salt
25g (1oz) vegetable margarine
25g (1oz) fresh yeast
15g (½oz) molasses
275ml (½pt) milk

Quick cheese bread (*makes 1 loaf*)
POWER LEVEL: 100% (FULL)

1 Lightly oil a deep 15–17.5cm (6–7in) round dish.
2 Mix the flour, baking powder, salt, pepper, mustard, herbs and cheese in a large bowl. Add the oil, egg and water, and mix to a soft dropping consistency.
3 Spoon the mixture into the prepared dish and cook, uncovered, for 6½–7 min. Allow to cool slightly, then turn out onto a rack. Serve sliced and spread with butter or sunflower margarine.

225g (8oz) wholewheat flour
1 × 5ml tsp (1tsp) baking powder
½ × 5ml tsp (½tsp) salt
freshly ground pepper
1 × 5ml tsp (1tsp) dried mustard
1 × 15ml tbsp (1tbsp) each freshly chopped chives and parsley
100g (4oz) farmhouse cheddar cheese, grated
2 × 15ml tbsp (2tbsp) sunflower oil
1 egg, beaten
150ml (¼pt) water

100g (4oz) butter
100g (4oz) light muscovado
  sugar
1 egg, beaten
175g (6oz) wholewheat flour
1 × 5ml tsp (1tsp) baking
  powder
75g (3oz) walnuts, finely
  chopped
150g (5oz) carob confectionery
  bar
25g (1oz) butter

Carob-coated walnut biscuits *(makes about 40)* *colour opposite*
POWER LEVEL: 100% (FULL)

1 Cream 100g (4oz) butter and sugar until light and fluffy, then gradually add the beaten egg. Fold in the flour, baking powder and walnuts to give a fairly stiff dough.
2 Turn onto a lightly floured board and shape into a roll, 27.5–30cm (11–12in) long. Wrap in clingfilm and chill for 1½–2 hr in the refrigerator.
3 Cut the rolls into 40 slices, approximately 6mm (¼in) thick. Cook the biscuits on a piece of greaseproof paper or baking parchment, 10 at a time, for 1¾–2 min. Transfer to a rack and leave until cold.
4 Break the carob bar into squares and place in a bowl. Heat for 2–3 min, or until melted. Add the 25g (1oz) butter, cut into slivers, and beat well.
5 Spread a little of the carob onto the back of each biscuit and leave until set.

2 eggs
50g (2oz) light muscovado
  sugar
65g (2½oz) fine wholewheat
  flour
1 × 15ml tbsp (1tbsp)
  sunflower oil
for decoration:
sugarless fruit spread or low-
  sugar jam, desiccated
  coconut

Wholewheat sponge cake *(serves 8)*
POWER LEVEL: 60%

1 Lightly oil a deep 17.5cm (7in) round cake dish.
2 Whisk together the eggs and sugar until foamy and really thick. This may take up to 10 min using an electric mixer. Fold in the flour and gradually add the oil down the side of the bowl. Fold in gently using a metal spoon, ensuring the flour and oil are well mixed in.
3 Pour the mixture into the prepared dish and cook for 4–5 min on 60% setting. Allow to stand for a few minutes before turning out onto a rack.
4 When cold, split and fill with sugarless fruit spread or jam. Sprinkle the top of the cake with a little desiccated coconut.

100g (4oz) butter or sunflower
  margarine
100g (4oz) light muscovado
  sugar
2 eggs, beaten
100g (4oz) wholewheat flour
2 × 5ml tsp (2tsp) baking
  powder
2 bananas, mashed
100g (4oz) walnuts, chopped
milk for mixing, optional

Banana and walnut cake *(serves 8–12)*
POWER LEVEL: 60% AND 100% (FULL)

1 Lightly oil a deep 17.5cm (7in) round cake dish and line the base with greaseproof paper or baking parchment.
2 Cream together the butter or margarine and sugar until light and fluffy, gradually add the eggs. Fold in the flour and baking powder, then the mashed bananas and walnuts. Add a little milk if necessary to give a soft consistency.
3 Turn the mixture into the prepared dish and cook, uncovered, for 8–10 min on 60% then a further 1–2 min on 100% (full) setting.
4 Allow to cool slightly before turning out onto a rack, then leave until cold.

75g (3oz) butter or sunflower
  margarine
50g (2oz) light muscovado
  sugar
3 × 15ml tbsp (3tbsp) honey
225g (8oz) rolled oats

Cheese and Orange Choux Buns (page 36); Honey Flapjacks (above); Carob-coated Walnut Biscuits (above)

Honey flapjacks *(serves 8)* *colour opposite*
POWER LEVEL: 100% (FULL) AND 60%

1 Line a shallow 20cm (8in) round dish with clingfilm.
2 Place the butter or margarine in a bowl with the sugar and honey. Heat for 1–2 min on 100 (full) setting, stirring occasionally, until the butter has melted and the sugar dissolved. Add the oats and mix well together.
3 Turn the mixture into the prepared dish and smooth the surface by pressing down with the back of a metal spoon.
4 Cook for 5–6 min on 60%. Allow to cool slightly, then remove from the dish onto a cooling rack. Mark into wedges and leave to cool completely.

114

rolled oats for sprinkling
275g (10oz) fine wholewheat
   flour
175g (6oz) rolled oats
1 × 5ml tsp (1tsp) salt
1 × 5ml tsp (1tsp) bicarbonate
   of soda
1 × 5ml tsp (1tsp) cream of
   tartar
100g (4oz) butter
1 × 15ml tbsp (1tbsp) light
   muscovado sugar
275ml (½pt) buttermilk or sour
   milk, approximately

1½ × 5ml tsp (1½tsp) dark
   muscovado sugar
425ml (¾pt) water,
   approximately
25g (1oz) fresh yeast
450g (1lb) granary meal
100g (4oz) wholewheat flour
1½ × 5ml tsp (1½tsp) salt
2 × 15ml tbsp (2tbsp) oil
nibbed wheat for sprinkling

Oaty soda bread (*cuts into 10 wedges*)
POWER LEVEL: 100% (FULL)

1 Lightly grease a 22.5cm (9in) round dish and line the base with grease-proof paper; sprinkle with oats.
2 Place the flour, oats, salt and raising agents in a bowl. Rub in the butter finely and mix in the sugar.
3 Add sufficient milk to give a light scone dough. Knead lightly on a floured surface and shape into a round about 2.5cm (1in) thick.
4 Place into the prepared container. Score or cut into 10 wedges and sprinkle the top with oats.
5 Cook for 5 min, turning once halfway through. Test with a skewer and give an extra minute if not quite cooked.
6 Leave for 10–15 min before turning onto a wire rack to cool.

Granary bread (*makes 1 loaf*)
POWER LEVEL: 100% (FULL)

1 Lightly grease a 22.5cm (9in) round dish or 900g (2lb) microwave loaf dish, and line the base with greaseproof paper.
2 Add the sugar to a third of the water and warm for 30 sec. Cream the yeast with this liquid and leave until frothy.
3 Mix the flours and salt well and warm for 30 sec. Warm the remaining liquid for 45 sec.
4 Add the yeast, oil and sufficient of the remaining liquid to the flour to form a soft dough. Mix well—very little kneading is required—and form into a ball.
5 Place the dough in a bowl covered with clingfilm, and prove by heating for 15 sec and leaving to stand for 5–10 min. Repeat this 3–4 times until doubled in size.
6 Turn the dough onto a lightly floured surface, knead well until smooth. Shape the dough, place in the prepared container, and prove as described previously until doubled in size.
7 Lightly oil the surface of the dough and sprinkle with nibbed wheat. Cut two deep cuts crossways over the top.
8 Cook for 5½–6½ min, turning once if necessary. Leave to stand for 10 min, then turn out onto a wire rack to cool.

Apricot slice *(cuts into 8–12 wedges)*
POWER LEVEL: 100% (FULL)

100g (4oz) dried apricots
boiling water
1 × 15ml tbsp (1tbsp) ground
  almonds
150g (5oz) sunflower margarine
150g (5oz) light muscovado
  sugar
150g (5oz) wholewheat flour
150g (5oz) rolled oats

1 Line a shallow 20cm (8in) round dish with clingfilm.
2 Place the apricots in a bowl and cover with boiling water. Cover the bowl and cook for 5 min. Allow to stand for 10–15 min.
3 Continue to cook the apricots for 5 min or until tender. Drain well and purée in a blender or food processor. Beat in the ground almonds.
4 Melt the margarine in a large bowl for 1½–2 min. Add the sugar, flour and oats and mix well.
5 Spoon half the oat mixture into the base of the prepared dish and press down with the back of a metal spoon. Spread the apricot purée over the oats, then top with the remaining mixture. Smooth the top.
6 Cook for 6–8 min. Allow to cool in the dish, then mark into wedges and transfer to a rack until completely cold. Store in an airtight tin.

Oatcakes *(makes 4)*
POWER LEVEL: 100% (FULL)

100g (4oz) medium oatmeal
pinch baking powder
pinch salt
15g (½oz) sunflower margarine
3 × 15ml tbsp (3tbsp) water
sunflower oil

These oatcakes are cooked in the browning dish

1 Place the oatmeal, baking powder and salt in a bowl.
2 Heat the margarine and water for approximately 1 min until the margarine is melted. Add to the oatmeal and mix well together.
3 Turn onto a board dredged with oatmeal and knead the dough lightly. Shape into a 17.5cm (7in) circle and cut into 4 wedges.
4 Preheat a browning dish for 6 min. Brush the dish lightly with oil and place the oatcakes on the dish. Cook for 1½ min, turn the cakes over and cook for a further 1 min. Place on a cooling rack.
5 Serve with cheese.

Wholewheat hot cross buns *(makes 12)*
POWER LEVEL: 100% (FULL)
CONVENTIONAL OVEN TEMPERATURE: 200°C (400°F) MARK 6

450g (1lb) wholewheat flour
1 × 5ml tsp (1tsp) salt
1 × 5ml tsp (1tsp) ground
  cinnamon
½ × 5ml tsp (½tsp) grated
  nutmeg
1 × 5ml tsp (1tsp) mixed spice
50g (2oz) light muscovado
  sugar
75g (3oz) currants
25g (1oz) chopped mixed peel
25g (1oz) fresh yeast
15g (½oz) light muscovado
  sugar
225ml (8fl oz) milk and water,
  mixed
1 egg, beaten
2 × 15ml tbsp (2tbsp)
  sunflower oil
25g (1oz) sunflower margarine
75g (3oz) wholewheat flour
6 × 15ml tbsp (6tbsp) water
honey for glaze

1 Place the 450g (1lb) flour, salt, spices, 50g (2oz) sugar, currants and peel in a large bowl and mix well together.
2 Mix the yeast with the 15g (½oz) sugar. Heat the milk and water for 45 sec or until tepid, and cream the yeast with a little of the liquid.
3 Stir the egg, oil, yeast liquid, remaining milk and water into the dry ingredients. Mix well to give a workable dough. Turn onto a floured board and knead until smooth.
4 Place the dough in a large bowl, cover and heat for 15 sec, then leave for 10—15 min. Repeat 4–5 times or until the dough is well risen.
5 Knock the dough back on a lightly floured board, divide into 12 pieces and shape into buns. Place the buns on two greased baking sheets.
6 Cover the baking sheets with clingfilm and leave in a warm place for 30–40 min until well risen.
7 Prepare the paste for the crosses by blending together the 25g (1oz) sunflower margarine, 75g (3oz) flour and the 6 × 15ml tbsp (6tbsp) water. Place the mixture into a piping bag fitted with a plain nozzle.
8 When the buns are risen, pipe a cross onto each one, then bake in the preheated oven for 20–25 min. As soon as the buns are cooked, brush each one with honey to give a glaze. Cool on a rack or eat warm.

Index

Roast Pheasant (page 56);
Bass with Spring Vegetables
(page 49)

Other microwave books by Val Collins

At last, in one handsome book, everything you need to know about microwave cookery—from a simple explanation of cooking techniques to a superb selection of recipes. Extensive information, delicious recipes, full colour photographs and delightful line drawings make it the one book every microwave cook will need. The recipes are to suit every taste, with detailed explanation of the methods to ensure the most delicious results.

Here is an ideal paperback that will give you all the background information you will need to become a microwave expert.

Val Collins explains in simple terms what microwave energy is and how it works. It is packed with ideas and appetising recipes too!

Probably more than any other food, fish benefits from being cooked by microwave as the moist texture and delicate flavour is preserved.

Val Collins provides a wealth of information and delicious recipes for a wide range of dishes: soups and starters; main courses such as haddock with orange and walnut stuffing and exotic dishes such as squid with mushrooms or scampi à la crème.

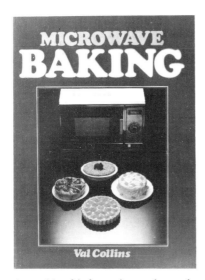

A wealth of information and mouth-watering recipes for the complete range of baking needs. Instructions are included for using conventional baking methods and combinations of microwave and conventional oven use.

Treat your family and friends to the real flavour of fruits and vegetables, cooked to perfection, looking and tasting better than those cooked by any other method. Details on freezing, blanching and drying herbs.